FIELDNOTES

ON FORTITUDE

Our Human Family, Inc., Orlando
ourhumanfamily.org
Copyright © 2025 by Our Human Family, Inc.
All rights reserved. Published 2025.

ISBN: 979-8-218-77278-9

PRINTED IN THE UNITED STATES OF AMERICA

10 9 8 7 6 5 4 3 2 1

Book and cover design by Clay Rivers

Cover photography by Nick Fancher, nickfancher.com

First Edition

FIELDNOTES

ON FORTITUDE

RESILIENCE IN RESISTANCE

Edited by
CLAY RIVERS
SHERRY KAPPEL
STEPHEN MATLOCK

OUR HUMAN FAMILY, INC.
Orlando
2025

For our ancestors.
For our descendants.
For ourselves.

*Humans are primed
to seek justice, fairness, and equity.
When something is amiss, we course correct
—or at least try our damnedest to.*
    –SHARON PENDANA

Contents

PREFACE

By CLAY RIVERS

SUMMER 2025. AMERICA is facing a profound break-down. The rise of extremist ideologies, the erasure of Black history from educational institutions, rampant cruelty and chaos, and the dismantling of government agencies threaten the fundamental rights and freedoms that once defined the nation. We witness a grim reality, where fear, outrage, and deep dismay are etched into the faces of many, like an epitaph on a headstone. The relentless stream of injustices outlined in the *Project*

2025 playbook is exacting a painful and incalculable toll, as intended.

On March 4, 2025, around eighty "50 States 50 Protests 1 Day" demonstrations took place in state capitols, courthouses, and city halls in all fifty states. After these protests, I was confronted with a pivotal question: *What are you going to do?*

I felt an urgent need to respond to the injustices unfolding around us, but participating in marches is not a viable option for me. Thankfully, I had alternative avenues for activism: writing and design. Moreover, I had connections with passionate writers and skilled editors around the country.

My answer to the pressing question was clear: publish an anthology to help people understand the current state of affairs and provide coping strategies for the overwhelming chaos of today's events. Drawing on my own life experiences, I appreciated the value of wise counsel and sought to craft this anthology, *Fieldnotes of Fortitude: Resilience in Resistance,* to assist others. Although the Our Human Family Board of Directors, Editorial Team, and I hadn't anticipated tackling a second anthology, we found ourselves eager to answer the call once again.

The aim of *Fieldnotes on Fortitude* is not to name specific policymakers, as individuals are already aware of who's pulling the levers. If they struggle to identify them, it often stems from their refusal to confront the truth. Instead, we will explore historical trends and first-person narratives honestly and respectfully, encouraging readers to absorb these accounts in a way that resonates with them.

The writers featured in this anthology were chosen for various reasons, with the fundamental criteria being their character as expressed through their writing. These writers are honest, treating their subjects and readers with care, and possess depth of knowledge and passion. They aim to connect with readers meaningfully, ensuring that those enduring these challenging times feel seen and valued.

Those addressing historical themes were selected for their expertise and their ability to convey knowledge effectively and within the context of the time period. Writers sharing personal narratives had to demonstrate storytelling skills, crafting concise accounts that reveal their lived experiences and emotional truths.

So, as we embark on this journey through *Fieldnotes of Fortitude: Resilience in Resistance,* our goal is to provide readers with the tools, insights, and support they need to navigate the current landscape. We aim to acknowledge the harsh realities while inspiring resilience and connection. Throughout this anthology, we hope to create a space for reflection and understanding, encouraging readers to engage with the material in a way that empowers them to act.

Fieldnotes on Fortitude: Resilience in Resistance has a simple through line, divided into five main sections:

1. Two Democracies Walk into a Bar
2. Authoritarianism in America

3. The Arc of the Moral Universe
4. Repealing the Twentieth Century
5. Resilience in Resistance

With the contributions of insightful writers and the richness of diverse experiences, this compilation stands as a testament to our collective struggle for justice and equality. Each narrative, whether personal or historical, adds to the tapestry of resilience. We invite every reader to reflect on their role within this tapestry and to consider how they can contribute to a future that honors our shared humanity and experiences.

As we move forward, let's embrace the power of our voices and the importance of community. Together, we can find ways to resist oppression and injustice, cultivating a brighter future for all.

The journey captured in *Fieldnotes of Fortitude* serves as a call to action, urging everyone to engage thoughtfully with the world around them. This anthology is not just a collection of writings; it is a manifesto of resilience, connection, and hope in the face of adversity.

Love one another.

Clay Rivers
August 30, 2025
Orlando, Florida

Clay Rivers is an author, award-winning artist, actor, and accidental activist. He is the president of the charitable organization Our Human Family, Inc., where he also serves as editorial director of its publications. Clay is a lector and lay eucharistic minister at his church in Orlando. He believes that society's ills can be solved by following Jesus's command to "love one another."

PART I

Two Democracies Walk into a Bar

Chapter 1

The Evolution of the MAGA Movement

By MICHAEL GREINER, PHD, JD

REPUBLICAN ACTIVISTS FREQUENTLY argue against the racist reputation of their party by pointing to its role in ending enslavement. They are correct. Indeed, the Republican Party was once known as the "party of emancipation," and public television's Fred Rogers, a devoted anti-racist, proudly pointed to his lifelong Republican voting record. Arguably, the most progressive president in history on racial justice issues was a Republican, Ulysses S. Grant,[1] and the former Confederacy made up the "solid south" for Democrats[2], home of the "yellow dog Democrats" who would rather vote for a dog than a Republican. As recently as 1976, Democrat Jimmy Carter won the South[3] by a commanding nine percentage points.

Similarly, Democrats, even seemingly progressive ones, embraced a racist agenda. Consider President Woodrow Wilson. The former president of Princeton University[4] is widely known for his advocacy of a League of Nations, a predecessor of the United Nations, that would allow countries to resolve their disputes peacefully rather than through war. He is less known, however, as the U.S. President who segregated[5] the federal government and appreciated the racist film *The Birth of a Nation*. His actions helped stall Black progress into the middle class for decades, earning him the enmity[6] of Black leaders such as W. E. B. Du Bois, the founder of the NAACP.

TRADING PLACES:
DEMOCRATS SHIFT TOWARD INCLUSIVITY

What the political commentators get wrong, however, is the idea that our current president is an aberration, that his open racism is a departure from the traditional inclusiveness of the Republican party. In fact, Donald Trump is the culmination of a process that started in the 1960s, and that by the 1980s was inevitable and predictable. For anyone who was paying close attention, a racist, white nationalist authoritarianism has been the destiny of the Republican party for the last fifty years.

Consider the political realities faced by the person often considered one of our most progressive presidents, Franklin Delano Roosevelt. With his left-leaning wife Eleanor[7] pushing him to action, he did indeed save American democracy and capitalism from the twin threats of the Great Depression and World War II. In so doing, however, he had to compromise with more conservative elements of his own party to hold the Democrats together. For example, to pass the Social Security Act, Roosevelt had to exclude railroad, agricultural, and domestic workers from its coverage. This seemingly arbitrary omission makes sense when one realizes that these fields were largely filled with Black workers. Indeed, these were among the few industries that historically provided opportunities for employment to Black people.[8] In other words, President Roosevelt's New Deal explicitly and purposely excluded Black people[9] from its benefits due to the committed racism of the Democratic party.

MICHAEL GREINER, PHD, JD

Democratic leaders from outside the old confederacy were likely uncomfortable with this position. Indeed, Roosevelt purportedly responded to entreaties for a more progressive agenda from A. Philip Randolph of the Black-dominated Brotherhood of Sleeping Car Porters by saying,[10] "You've convinced me. I agree with what you've said. Now go out and make me do it." Thus, while President Roosevelt was likely sympathetic with an anti-racist agenda, he was not willing to get ahead of public opinion on this issue.

Over time, however, the incompatibility of racism

with progressive, pro-worker policies became unsustainable. The first cracks in the Democratic commitment to racism likely occurred during the administration of President Harry S. Truman. The "Accidental President,"[11] looked down upon with disdain by the eastern establishment elite who made up the Roosevelt administration, and often considered relatively conservative with his anti-communist foreign policy,[12] Truman was the President who desegregated the military with his executive order number 9981.[13] While many felt Truman moved too slowly to address racial inequality, this executive order from 1948 was likely the first step toward a more inclusive Democratic party.

KENNEDY EMBRACES BLACK VOTERS

Later, in 1960, after Republicans held the White House for nearly a decade, northeastern Catholic liberal John F. Kennedy made an appeal for Black votes in his desperate attempt to win one of the closest presidential elections in history. A few weeks before the November election, a Georgia court sentenced the Rev. Dr. Martin Luther King Jr. to hard labor and solitary confinement for participating in a peaceful sit-in. In response, President Kennedy called Dr. King's wife Coretta, then six months pregnant, to offer his support.[14] While in retrospect this seems like an insignificant action, it helped galvanize Black support behind Kennedy. And while some Kennedy advisers worried that white voters would be offended, they could rest assured that the Solid South would stay behind the Democrat, because white voters of the era refused to vote for anybody nominated by the Republicans, the party of emancipation.

Kennedy's action during the campaign presaged an administration that would demonstrate a strong commitment to end racism.[15] It was during his administration that efforts were made to integrate buses and universities, with Kennedy sending federal marshals and mobilizing the National Guard to protect Black people trying to avail themselves of these services. But Kennedy's efforts were hampered by his relative lack of legislative experience, having only been elected to the U.S. Senate in 1952, and serving the entire time as the junior senator from Massachusetts. Ironically, this would all change upon his assassination in 1963, when the southerner, former Senate Majority Leader Lyndon B. Johnson, would take his place.

MICHAEL GREINER, PHD, JD

JOHNSON USHERS IN THE CIVIL RIGHTS ERA

Johnson was cut from an entirely different mold from Kennedy. While Kennedy was a Harvard-educated Pulitzer prize-winning author from a wealthy family, Johnson grew up poor, graduating from a state college in Texas.[16] He rose in politics through his wits and hard work, with no family money to help him. Due to his background as a southern Democrat, most expected Johnson to espouse the racist policies of his party. But if Johnson had any defining characteristic, it was his compassion.[17] Elected to Congress in 1937 at just twenty-nine years of age, Johnson was known for his steadfast support of Roosevelt's New Deal.[18] These policies, however, did not require Johnson to put his position on racial equality on the record. That would all change once Johnson got to the White House.

A little-known fact about Lyndon Johnson was that he spent his early years working as a teacher in a impoverished, segregated Mexican-American school in the South Texas town of Cotulla.[19] His experience there left him with a deep commitment to education, as well as empathy for people who were discriminated against because of the color of their skin. Once President, Johnson found he could finally do something about the inequities he witnessed.

Additionally, like Truman before him, Johnson was disdained by Kennedy's Ivy-educated team.[20] Like Truman, he was viewed as an accidental president who shared no elite attributes with his predecessor. This disrespect hurt Johnson, prompting him to try to win over his critics by doubling down on Kennedy's policies.[21] If Kennedy sent military advisers to Vietnam, Johnson would fully commit the U.S. military. If Kennedy supported racial equality, Johnson would pass the most important civil rights legislation in American history: the Civil Right Acts of 1964 and the Voting Rights Act of 1965. Johnson was buoyed in his effort with a commanding electoral victory in 1964 against Senator Barry Goldwater that left him with a Democratic supermajority in both houses of Congress.[22]

Johnson, however, operated under no illusions. He

knew that Goldwater was a weak candidate who repelled many voters with his aggressive foreign policy at a time when many feared nuclear war. He also knew that of the six states he lost, five of them were part of the once "Solid South," indicating that the Democrats' once unassailable, white supremacist hold on that region was weakening. The reason for this region's change away from loyalty to the Democrats was obvious: racism. Johnson knew it. After passing the Civil Rights Act, Johnson quipped to his press secretary privately, "I think we may have lost the south for your lifetime—and mine."[23] Johnson was a consummate politician, and his prediction was prescient. He would be the last Democratic candidate for president to win the white vote.[24]

MICHAEL GREINER, PHD, JD

NIXON AND THE GOP SHIFT RIGHT

For their part, Democrats took a moral stand. They came to believe that a party emphasizing justice and fairness could not simultaneously support racism. Had the Republicans continued to stand against racism, America might have moved to a post-racial society. But the Republican party was about to be redefined by a cynical politician who saw opportunity with a "southern strategy."[25] That candidate was Richard Nixon, and in 1968 he won the election by appealing directly to the frustrations racist southern white people had with the Democratic Party's move to support inclusivity.

Nixon conceived the strategy of using "dog-whistles" to appeal to white voters' racism without explicitly using racist words.[26] As H. R. Haldeman, Nixon's close adviser, said, "The key is to devise a system that recognizes this while not appearing to."[27] According to historian Robert Brent Toplin, "Rather than refer directly to blacks, Nixon promised 'law and order' and respect for 'states' rights.'"[28] The strategy worked, with Nixon winning the presidency after losing it in 1960, and receiving his highest level of support in the South.[29]

This cynical "dog whistling" approach only took the Republicans so far. In the 1968 election, Nixon lost several states in the Deep South to George Wallace,[30] who ran at the head of the American Independent Party. Wallace, of course, was the infamous governor of Alabama who blocked Black students from entering the University of Alabama. In his 1963 inaugural address, he proclaimed his support for "segregation now, segregation tomorrow, and segregation forever,"[31] and in 1970 unseated an incumbent governor with a campaign President Jimmy Carter, a southerner himself, called "one of the most racist campaigns in modern southern political history."[32] This was the kind of racism these states of the former confederacy wanted, but it was too much for the rest of the country at the time, leading to the election of Nixon, who left the racism coded.

One cannot overestimate the cynicism of Richard Nixon. This was the President who presided over an effort to steal documents from the offices of the Democratic National Committee, located in the Watergate building in Washington.[33] When the burglars hired by Nixon bungled the operation, he worked for years to cover up his involvement. And when former Pentagon analyst Daniel Ellsberg released to the press a report detailing the deceit underpinning the Vietnam War, Nixon ordered his reputation smeared and sued *The New York Times* in an attempt to discredit the leak.[34] Nothing would stand in the way of Nixon's quest for power.

Nixon's strategy became the model for subsequent successful Republican presidential candidates. His former Vice President, Gerald Ford, who replaced Nixon in the wake of the Watergate scandal, refused to engage in this kind of race-baiting. The result was his defeat by Democrat Jimmy Carter. Republicans would not make the same mistake again. When Ronald Reagan ran in 1980, he told stories about welfare queens who used food stamps to purchase T-bone steaks. He also professed his support for "state's rights," the purported justification for the confederate rebellion. By making racist statements without explicitly singling out Black people, this approach provided a convenient deniability for otherwise racist appeals.

George H.W. Bush, Reagan's Vice President, would follow the same roadmap, running an ad featuring Black men getting weekend prison passes.[35] The basis for the ad was a tragic incident in which a prisoner, Willie Horton, during a prison furlough committed a murder and rape while Democratic candidate Mike Dukakis was governor of Massachusetts. George Bush's campaign manager Lee Atwater stated that his goal was to make voters think "Willie Horton is Michael Dukakis's running mate."[36] The cynicism of the ad was evidenced by

MICHAEL GREINER, PHD, JD

the fact that all fifty states had a similar prison furlough program in place, including one supported by then-President and former California governor Ronald Reagan.[37] Bush also was known as being relatively supportive of racial equality. None of that mattered, however, when power was at stake. Even Bush's adviser Atwater would ultimately admit that this approach was wrong,[38] albeit successful for a time.

Ultimately, however, this approach would prove unsustainable for Republicans. At some point, their racist supporters demanded more than just occasional rhetorical flourishes in support of their position—they wanted action. As they saw it, they voted again and again for candidates who promised to stop progress toward racial equality; despite this, society seemed to be getting more and more open and diverse. This lack of progress on their racist priority angered them.

AMERICANS CHOOSE SIDES ON RACISM

This anger came to a head when America elected its first Black President, Barack Obama. No longer would coded racism be sufficient to satisfy the resentments of racist white voters. This is where Donald Trump stepped in, embracing the false narrative that Obama was not born in the United States,[39] and calling Mexican immigrants "rapists."[40] And unlike other Republican presidents, his racism would affect government policy, with a recent White House release touting his efforts to remove "killers, rapists and drug dealers from our streets" as part of "the largest criminal illegal immigrant deportation operation in American history."[41] Finally, here was a Republican the racists could really get behind.

The expectations among the racist crowd would not have been disappointed had it not been for the Republicans fanning their resentments through forty years of campaigns. In so doing, the Republican candidates were playing with fire, allowing racist anger to grow fed by the rhetoric they used on the campaign trail. At some point, the racists would demand their due. After all, they had supported the Republican candidates who mouthed their priorities. Now they wanted to see the halting progress enjoyed by Black people and other marginalized groups finally put to an end. This progress was symbolized by the Obama presidency, and the racists were tired of waiting.

Even in the 1980s, the danger of the Republican embrace of racism was evident to many. Famously, then Senator Edward M. Kennedy voiced this concern in his speech opposing Reagan's nomination of Robert Bork to the Supreme Court. "Robert Bork's America is a land in which women would be forced into back-alley abortions, blacks would sit at segregated lunch counters, rogue police could break down citizens' doors in midnight raids, schoolchildren could not be taught about evolution, writers and artists would be censored at the whim of government, and the doors of the federal courts would be shut on the fingers of millions of citizens for whom the judiciary is often the only protector of the individual rights that are the heart of our democracy,"

MICHAEL GREINER, PHD, JD

Kennedy argued.[42] While Bork's nomination was ultimately defeated, the vision he espoused has become all too true in the person of Donald Trump. It just took the racist conservatives longer to achieve their goal than they had originally hoped.

We could belabor this analysis by discussing each presidential election since 1988, but they would just reveal more of the same: using racism as a means to achieve power. Even Mitt Romney, the Republican presidential nominee against Barack Obama in 2012, who had been a relatively progressive governor of Massachusetts, helping pass health care legislation that was the inspiration behind Obamacare, resorted to racist appeals.[43] Trump's racist appeals are simply a continuation of what we have seen in the past, just dialed up in response to the growing frustration of racist white voters.

Each Republican administration delivered just enough racism to satisfy the racists and keep them in power; it's just that after the election of a Black president, those demands have increased exponentially. In fact, there are a number of parallels between Richard Nixon, the originator of this strategy, and our current President. Both share an unbridled sense of greed and lust for power. Both exhibit a disdain for the rule of law and a belief that the machinery of government can be used to intimidate political critics. Both assail the courts which seek to constrain their quest for power while also repeatedly engaging in questionable litigation to bully those who dare oppose him. No, Trump is not an aberration; he is the next step in a line that runs from Richard Nixon in 1968 through Reagan, Bush, and even Mitt Romney, directly to him.

Will Rogers famously quipped "I am not a member of any organized political party; I am a Democrat."[44] For a time, it seemed as if this truism might have finally run its course. After all, in the wake of Trump's defeat in 2020, Republicans appeared in disarray while the progressive wing of the Democratic party was firmly on board with President Joe Biden's agenda. But since the 2024 election, it seems as if Rogers's observation is once again apt. The Democrats seem lost and discouraged while Republicans display a remarkable level of unity.

MICHAEL GREINER, PHD, JD

The problem is simple, however: it is harder to organize people around a message of inclusivity than one of greed and lust for power. After all, by definition, greed and lust for power give the people something in return for their support, and racism is a useful tool to achieve these goals. On the other hand, inclusivity by definition means that people come together with different backgrounds, priorities, and values. Often, these goals will conflict with each other, resulting in one of both groups abandoning the coalition—just as we saw in the recent split between Jewish voters and those with Palestinian sympathies.

The advantage Trump brings such a coalition is a common enemy to unify against. The disadvantage is that once Trumpism has been removed from office, the coalition splits, as we saw in the wake of the 2020 election. Despite calls by some Republicans to abandon their use of racism as a tool to achieve power,[45] the easier, more consistently successful strategy is to simply double down on racism. This approach has helped keep the Republicans relevant despite the growing diversity of the American population. The danger is that each time the Democratic coalition cracks, a Republican comes into power who must deliver an even more toxic dose of racism than the one before. One can only wonder, and fear, what comes after Trump.

Michael Greiner, PhD, JD, has managed political campaigns across the country, worked on Capitol Hill, and served as Deputy Mayor of Warren, Michigan's third largest city. His firm, specializing in bankruptcy law, has helped thousands of families and businesses restructure their debts. His research has been published in *The Harvard Business Review, The Journal of Business Strategy, The Journal of Business Research,* and other top journals.

MICHAEL
GREINER,
PHD, JD

Chapter 2

Death by Demagogue: How Democracies End

By Glenn Rocess

EVERYONE WANTS TO matter. This notion is every bit as valid for the newborn child crying for the warmth of her mother as it is for the older adult living out their final days in a long-term care facility. We all want to be of some positive value in the eyes of others, for our voices to be heard, and to make a difference in the world. The inherent worth of every individual is the appeal of democracy: that our presence and voice are relevant, whether we're one of a half-dozen children deciding what game to play, one of a thousand workers unionizing for better working conditions, or one of a hundred million voters deciding the political fate of their nation.

To paraphrase Thomas Jefferson, such a truth is not just self-evident, but an unalienable right. Unfortunately, as the prophet Daniel pointed out to King Nebuchadnezzar over 2,500 years ago, we all have proverbial feet of clay that reveal our personal character weaknesses. This foible is the challenge facing the real-world implementation of democracy: It sounds great on paper, but the shortcomings of human psychology ensure that the very devil is in the details.

HOW DEMOCRACIES OF THE PAST DIED

THE MOTHER OF DEMOCRACY. The earliest recorded democracies appear to be the sixteen republics of ancient India's *Mahajanapadas* from as early as the sixth century BCE,[3] over one hundred years before the Greek statesman Cleisthenes implemented *demokratia* or "people power," in Athens. The Mahajanapadas' style of government was termed *gana sanghas*, which translates to "people's assemblies." Their governments were not as we understand democracy today, but they nonetheless practiced collective rule, decentralized power structures, and elected leadership.[4] For this reason, India's current prime minister Narendra Modi refers to his nation as the "Mother of Democracy,"[5] despite his own strong authoritarian tendencies.[6]

Because of their decentralized governments, the

Mahajanapadas experienced internal strife but were unable to unite against external threats from nearby monarchies with strong militaries and centralized bureaucracies, similar to the challenges faced by Ukraine and Taiwan today.

ATHENS. Athens' fame as the first great Western democracy is probably due to the wealth of surviving information available from historians such as Thucydides, Aristotle, and Plato. The city-state's long and painful journey to democracy began in 621 BCE, and they eventually instituted a political system that included legislation and executive orders, and in which all adult free male citizens were eligible to participate, depending upon their level of income. Otherwise the Athenian system of suffrage resembled America's passage of our Nineteenth Amendment that granted women the right to vote.

Any discussion of Athenian demokratia must include the fact that their system of government was essentially experimental. There was little precedent and no indication they knew of any other nation that had ever made a serious effort at democracy. In fact, Socrates and his student Plato both argued against such an endeavor. In their judgment, the majority of the people, because they were by and large ignorant and unskilled, would always get it wrong. In these intellectuals' view, government was an art, craft, or skill, and should be entrusted only to the skilled and intelligent, who were by definition a minority.[7]

But perhaps the most perceptive argument against democracy was made by Aristotle, who warned of the peril presented by the demagogue:

> And these [demagogues] cause the resolutions of the assembly [of the masses] to be supreme and not the laws, by referring all things to the people; for they owe their rise to greatness to the fact that the people [are] sovereign over all things while they are sovereign over the opinion of the people, for the multitude believes them.[8]

Before proceeding further, we should define the demagogue. According to historian Reinhard Luthin, a demagogue is defined as:

> . . . a politician skilled in oratory, flattery and invective; evasive in discussing vital issues; promising everything to everybody; appealing to the passions rather than the reason of the public; and arousing racial, religious, and class prejudices—a man whose lust for power without recourse to principle leads him to seek to become a master of the masses. He has for centuries practiced his profession of 'man of the people'. He is a product of a political tradition nearly as old as western civilization itself.[9]

Aristotle's words rang true with the advent of a demagogue named Cleon of Athens. He was "an effective, if vulgar, speaker . . . given to extravagant promises and prodigious accusations against opponents"[10] who set himself against Pericles, the popular leader of Athens known to be a wise and honorable statesman.[11]

Pericles led Athens through the first half of the Peloponnesian War against Sparta, but he succumbed to a plague. Cleon then rose to the forefront of Athenian politics and convinced Athens to engage in military adventurism that decimated their army and bankrupted the nation's coffers. After several more years of war Athens was defeated by Sparta.[12]

The downfall of Athens' democracy was due to three factors: first, the hubris of Pericles and the other leaders of Athens who took their city down the path to war with Sparta. Second, the rise of Cleon, whose hatred of Sparta prevented any hope of compromise or effective diplomacy. Third, and perhaps the most important factor in this list, the Athenian democracy did not have enforced legal safeguards in place that might have stopped Cleon from hijacking the government and the will of the people.

ROME. Rome's own journey towards democracy began in 509 BCE when Lucius Junius Brutus expelled Tarquin Superbus, the last king of Rome, and founded the Roman Republic. The Republic lasted until 27 BCE when Gaius Julius Caesar Augustus, also known as Octavian, defeated the combined fleets of Cleopatra and Mark Antony at the battle of Actium and proclaimed himself "First Citizen" of the Roman Empire.

The key in the preceding paragraph isn't that the Roman Republic was dissolved and placed under imperial rule, but that it had lasted nearly half a millennium before it fell, during which time its borders had spread from the coastal hinterlands of the Italian peninsula to include most of the lands surrounding the Mediterranean Sea, all of modern-day France, and much of Britain.

What made the Roman Republic so successful? One could point to their great military, their vast economy, and the comprehensive infrastructure that enabled both. But none of those would have been possible without a stable, functioning government. The Romans had adopted what the Greek historian Polybius termed a "mixed constitution." In his view, "the ideal government should combine elements of monarchy, aristocracy, and democracy, with each element serving as a check on the others."[13] This separation of powers was put into practice by Rome with their consuls, senators, and tribunes.

Many readers will immediately see the similarity between Polybius's monarchy, aristocracy, and democracy and today's American government consisting of the presidency, the Senate, and the House of Representatives. This is not a coincidence; indeed, the Framers of the U.S. Constitution deliberately considered Polybius' statements concerning the separation of powers during the Constitutional Convention of 1787.[14]

The Roman Republic's fall began with unchecked political partisanship that culminated with the assassination of Gaius Julius Caesar. In the month before his assassination, Caesar had himself declared *dictator perpetuo*, literally "dictator for life," in direct violation of the Roman constitution. When the Roman Senate tried to rescind some of his dictatorial power and authority, he simply ignored them.[15] According to historian Barry Strauss, Caesar believed the rule of law no longer applied to himself, and that "only his genius offered the people of the empire peace and prosperity."[16] In other words, Julius Caesar was a demagogue of the highest order.

THE IGBO DEMOCRACY

Democracy was never limited to Asia and Europe. After all, the desire for self-determination is a human trait not limited by ethnicity or geography. The Igbo people of modern-day Nigeria had one of the purest forms of democracy prior to the Industrial Era. Here from a 1973 interview are the words of Noo Udala, an Igbo man who at age 102 provided this description of the Igbo form of democracy:

> Before the white man came we had no chief that saw to the affairs of the town. But we had several institutions that helped us organise [sic] our activities. The government of this town was not vested in one man . . . During any cases affecting the whole town, the *ndi ishi ani*, village heads, would meet and discuss effectively the

23

issues involved. They met as equals though at times preference was given to the village head from this village, Umunnacha, as we are the oldest village. But before any decision was carried, the issue must have been agreed on by all. After arriving at this decision, each village head would go home to discuss decisions with their respective communities.[17]

The Igbo form of representative democracy provided a great deal of local and personal freedom; however, the lack of a strong centralized government nearly always results in weakness against foreign powers. In the case of the Igbo democracy, they faced the overwhelming might of the British colonizers whose policies enabled the deeper societal ravages of chattel enslavement and European missionaries.

In *Things Fall Apart*, his novel about the end of the Igbo democracy, Chinua Achebe wrote, " . . . the arrival of white missionaries and colonial [administration] gradually destroyed that traditional life of Igbo people from within by grinding down its value system, firstly through piece-meal religious conversions [in] place of the traditional Igbo one."[18]

The implication is clear that the societal damage wrought by colonizers and missionaries continues and is a primary cause of the societal conflicts and political instability endemic to sub-Saharan Africa today.

FRANCE: THE DIRECTORATE. In 1789, less than two
months after America's Constitutional Convention began
in Philadelphia, the people of Paris revolted and stormed
the Bastille, the prison that had become a symbol of
royal tyranny. Less than three years later, King Louis
XIV himself was brought before Robespierre's ironically
named Committee of Public Safety, found guilty of trea-
son, and guillotined.[19] Soon after began the Reign of
Terror during which tens of thousands were executed
out-of-hand, usually for the suspicion that they were
enemies of the Revolution.

The Terror ended in 1794 with the death of Robespierre, when the survivors from the moneyed and
influential class formed the Directorate. It included a
bicameral legislature with an upper and lower house.
The upper house—the Council of Ancients—chose five
individuals as directors to serve as the executive branch
of the fledgling democracy. But in reaction to the hom-
icidal rule suffered under the Reign of Terror, the Directors themselves were kept politically weak and were
not even allowed the funding to enforce the measures
they believed necessary to stabilize the badly fractured
French society.[20]

What followed was four years of widespread political instability during which France still became mired
in wars against Britain, Russia, Prussia, and several

GLENN
ROCESS

other nations and principalities. These wars combined to wreck the French economy and further diminish the public's trust in the Directorate, thus opening the way for Napoleon Bonaparte who, like Julius Caesar before him, was a military genius and a great reformer who believed that he alone could restore France to continental supremacy, and that the rule of law did not apply to him. Napoleon's hubris is best exemplified by his choice of "First Citizen" as his title, the same title claimed by the first emperor of Rome 1,800 years before.

RUSSIA: THE KERENSKY REPUBLIC. In 1917 there was not one, but two Russian revolutions. The first came in February of that year with the culmination of the people's dissatisfaction with the incompetence of Tsar Nicholas II whose missteps had resulted in food shortages, a deeply unpopular war, and a government too weak to effectively maintain order. In an interesting parallel to France's Reign of Terror, he had even created a Department of the Protection of Public Safety and Order, an organization of spies and secret police that performed functions similar to Robespierre's Committee of Public Safety.[22]

Tsar Nicholas II realized he had lost popular support and agreed to abdicate. But his offer was too little and too late. He and his entire family were arrested before they could flee the country, imprisoned in a cellar, and executed in July of that year.[23]

The Duma (Congress) moved quickly to form a provisional government on democratic principles.

Under Aleksandr Kerensky, the Provisional Government "instituted freedoms of speech, press, assembly, and religion; universal suffrage; and equal rights for women."[24] Unfortunately, Vladimir Lenin—long known as a revolutionary demagogue—had been secretly transported by Germany into Russia to destabilize the Russian government. Lenin's nearly instant political rise was reported in a message from Germany's top army command to Berlin's foreign office: "Lenin's entry into Russia was a success. He is working according to your wishes."[25]

With the promise of "peace, land, and bread," Lenin and the Bolsheviks gained the support of enough of the military and the peasants to overthrow the Provisional Government[26] and force Kerensky to flee the country.

Despite the Provisional Government's support of democratic freedoms and principles, the Russian Republic never really stood a chance. The nation was wracked by hunger, political chaos, and war, and the Bolsheviks —too popular and well-entrenched to eliminate—were determined to take control of the nation for themselves.

GERMANY: THE WEIMAR REPUBLIC. When the Weimar Republic is mentioned, the first thing that comes to mind is hyperinflation and the pictures of a wheelbarrow of Papiermarks—the currency of the Weimar Republic— just to purchase a loaf of bread. It is true that at its worst point, the Papiermark-to-U.S. dollar exchange rate was 4.2 *trillion* to one. What is less well-known is that the Weimar Republic recovered from hyperinflation and became prosperous by the late 1920s. Germany was well on its way to regaining "great power" status with a stable representative democracy that guaranteed more personal and economic freedoms than could be found in the United States.[27]

Two factors doomed the Weimar Republic. First and foremost was the Treaty of Versailles, the grossly unfair document Germany was forced to sign at the end of World War I. French General Ferdinand Foch said of the treaty, "This is not peace. It is an armistice for twenty years."[28] Twenty years, two months, and three days after the treaty was signed, Nazi Germany invaded Poland, and World War II began.

The second factor was the economic collateral damage wrought by America's Great Depression. German unemployment skyrocketed and fear of a return to hyperinflation was widespread. As is so often the case in such times, the one who seemed strongest, promised the most to the voting public, and pointed to a certain demographic to blame for the nation's woes—the demagogue Adolf Hitler—legally rose to power as chancellor of Germany.[29]

Looking at the three modern democracies above, short-lived as they all were, one can see a common thread. These democracies in France, Russia, and Germany all formed in times of deep political instability following a major war, and all three fell when deep economic crisis combined with political instability to enable the rise of a popular and larger-than-life demagogue.

Indeed, the same fate befell both Athens and Rome: at a time of crisis, a popular demagogue rose to seize power. We do not know if such led to the fall of the Indian Mahajanapadas republics, but in the case of the Igbo democracies, one might even consider state-sponsored evangelization of religion—complete with the promises, blame, and force of arms mentioned earlier—as a form of organized demagoguery. That brings us back full circle to Aristotle's warning that the problem with democracy is that a demagogue will eventually rise to convince the people that they are sovereign over all things, even as they themselves are unwittingly enthralled to his will.

COMMON FLAWS, BUT UNCOMMON STRENGTHS

The above examples make clear how democracies can fail, how easily national government under democratic principles is imperiled by demagoguery enabled by economic crisis, weak central authority, and political instability. Interestingly enough, failure to unite against a foreign enemy is the least common factor of all. Germany's example also shows that even strict adherence to the rule of law is no guarantee of a democracy's success.

Nevertheless, as can be seen by the examples of Switzerland, the United Kingdom, and the United States, democracies can last for centuries even as they bring social and economic prosperity to their populations. What do these nations—and all other successful first-world democracies—have in common? In one way or another, they all utilize the system of "mixed constitution" (also known as "mixed government") described by Polybius: the combination of elements of monarchy, aristocracy, and democracy.

Having such mixed government is not a panacea for all the ills of the political world. In fact, it seems that one other thing successful democracies have in common is the near-constant ire of the people over the issues of the day. No matter what the government does, there will be those who vociferously oppose it. The difference, of course, is the degree of dissatisfaction by a nation's population concerning the issues at hand.

While the democratic process has its share of endless frustrating challenges, it is worth pointing out quite rightly that democracy is nonetheless the very best form of government yet devised in recorded human history, in comparison to other forms of government humanity has devised over the centuries.

Glenn Rocess is retired Navy, has traveled five continents, and has worn many hats, including as a steam plant supervisor, LAN admin, OSHA inspector, foster parent of medically fragile children, and an adult family home owner. More importantly, he is a dad, a husband of thirty-three years, and fears absolutely nothing except his wife's guilt trips.

REFERENCES

1. Margaritoff, Marco (2017, June 30). 7 Disturbing Facts About Thomas Jefferson, From Racism To Rape. https://allthatsinteresting.com/thomas-jefferson-dark-side

2. Wills, Garry (2003, January 1). "Negro president' – Jefferson and the slave power." https://archive.org/details/negropresident jeoooowill_j5v0

3. Editors of Encyclopedia Britannica. (1998, July 20) Diodorus Siculus, Greek Historian. https://www.britannica.com/biography/Diodorus-Siculus

4. Pulakesh (2024, December 8). Republics (Gana-Sanghas) in Ancient India and Their Significance. https://upscanswer.com/republics-gana-sanghas-in-ancient-india-and-their-significance/

5. Fuchs, Sandhya (2024, April 11). The authoritarian leader's playbook: how Narendra Modi captured India's legal system and is rewriting the country's history in his image. https://theconversation.com/the-authoritarian-leaders-playbook-how-narendra-modi-captured-indias-legal-system-and-is-rewriting-the-countrys-history-in-his-image-226889

6. The Economic Times Editorial Bureau (2023, March 29). India mother of democracy; home to idea of elected leaders much before rest of world: PM Modi. https://economictimes.indiatimes.com/news/politics-and-nation/india-mother-of-democracy-home-to-idea-of-elected-leaders-much-before-rest-of-world-pm-modi/articleshow/99089898.cms

7. Cartledge, Paul (2011, February 17) Critics and Critiques of Athenian Democracy. https://www.bbc.co.uk/history/ancient/greeks/greekcritics_01.shtml

8. Aristotle (4th Century BCE). Politics. https://www.perseus.

tufts.edu/hopper/text?doc=Perseus:text:1999.01.c058:book=4:section=1292a

9. Luthin, Reinhard Henry (1954). American Demagogues: 20th Century. https://archive.org/details/americandemagoguoooluth/page/2/mode/2up

10. Gomme, Cadoux, and Rhodes (2015, December 22). Cleon. https://oxfordre.com/classics/display/10.1093/acrefore/9780199381135.001.0001/acrefore-9780199381135-e-1666

11. Lewis, David Malcom (2025, March 18). Pericles. https://www.britannica.com/biography/Pericles-Athenian-statesman/The-drift-toward-war

12. The Editors of Encyclopedia Britannica (2025, May 12). Peloponnesian War. https://www.britannica.com/event/Peloponnesian-War

13. World History Edu (2023, May 11). Polybius: The Greek historian who explained how the Roman Republic came to be great. https://worldhistoryedu.com/polybius-the-greek-historian-who-explained-how-the-roman-republic-came-to-be-great/

14. Lloyd, Marshall Davies (1998, September 22). Polybius and the Founding Fathers: the separation of powers. https://mlloyd.org/mdl-indx/polybius/polybius.htm

15. Fife, Steven (2012, January 18). The Brothers Gracchi: The Tribunates of Tiberius and Gaius Gracchus. https://www.worldhistory.org/article/95/the-brothers-gracchi-the-tribunates-of-tiberius--g/

16. Strauss, Barry S. (2015). The Death of Caesar: The Story of History's Most Famous Assassination. https://archive.org/details/deathofcaesarstooooostra

17. Isichei, Elizabeth (1978). Igbo Worlds: An Anthology of Oral Histories and Historical Descriptions. Included as a resource for Trask, David (2004, May 1). Biafra, Nigeria, the West and the World. https://www.historians.org/resource/igbo-village-democracy/

18. Dr. Pooja (2022, April 4). A Study of Colonial Confrontation in The Things Fall Apart of Chinua Achebe's. https://ijcrt.org/papers/IJCRT2204535.pdf

19. Lovejoy, Paul E. and Hogendorn, Jan S. (1993, August 27). Slow Death for Slavery: The Course of Abolition in Northern Nigeria 1897-1936 (African Studies, Series Number 76) https://archive.org/details/slowdeathforslavoopaul/page/n3/mode/2up

20. The Editors of Encyclopedia Britannica (2025, April 21). French Revolution. https://www.britannica.com/event/French-Revolution

21. The Editors of Encyclopedia Britannica (2023, September 19). Directory. https://www.britannica.com/topic/Directory-French-history

22. Fischer, Ben B. (1997). Okhrana: The Paris Operations of the Russian Imperial Police. https://www.cia.gov/resources/csi/static/Okhrana-The-Paris-Operations.pdf

23. Keep, John L. H. (2025, May 14). Nicholas II. https://www.britannica.com/biography/Nicholas-II-tsar-of-Russia

24. The Editors of the Encyclopedia Britannica (2025, April 28). Aleksandr Kerensky. https://www.britannica.com/biography/Aleksandr-Kerensky

25. Wagener, Volker (2017, July 11). Germany's role in the Russian Revolution. https://www.dw.com/en/how-germany-got-the-russian-revolution-off-the-ground/a-41195312

26. The Editors of Encyclopedia Britannica (2025, May 4). The February Revolution: Kerensky and the Kornilov revolt. https://www.britannica.com/event/Russian-Revolution/The-February-Revolution#ref348363

27. The Editors of Encyclopedia Britannica (2025, April 29). Weimar Republic. https://www.britannica.com/place/Weimar-Republic

28. History.com Editors (2025, May 27). Ferdinand Foch. https://www.history.com/articles/ferdinand-foch

29. (author and date not listed). End of the Weimar Republic – Welsh Joint Education Committee. The impact of the Depression on Germany. https://www.bbc.co.uk/bitesize/guides/zp34srd/revision/1

PART II

Authoritarianism in America

Chapter 3

From Reconstruction to Redemption

By William F. Spivey

M Y TWELVE-YEAR-OLD GRANDDAUGHTER called me to ask if segregation was returning. She thought I would be the one to ask that question. She had watched five separate videos on YouTube from white people wanting segregation to return. I explained she shouldn't worry about it. Just because some white people feel that way doesn't mean it's likely to happen.

After we hung up, I considered all the forces trying to segregate America in various ways, let alone those wanting to start a race war. The widespread resistance to

integrating Black and white people began with Reconstruction and has advanced in fits and starts, sometimes
retreating. The battle must continue, or the Redemption movement might have the last word. I realize I just
discredited hundreds of individual and group acts of
resistance that occurred earlier, including the German
Coast Rebellion, the Nat Turner Revolt, the Gabriel
Prosser Rebellion, the Denmark Vesey Revolt, and the
Stono Rebellion.

RECONSTRUCTION

I submit that the Reconstruction Era was the first national effort to promote equality and integrate Black people into most facets of society. Christian organizations
and the Republican Party supported these efforts in what
could be described as diversity, equity, and inclusion for
lack of better words.

Understanding Reconstruction requires an appreciation of what things were like at the end of the Civil War.
Four million enslaved people were purportedly freed
across the South at the end of the war. Some were techni-
cally freed by the Emancipation Proclamation on January
1, 1863, provided they could reach free territory. Many
were illiterate due to the intentional effort to keep them
from communicating.

In particular, enslaved people weren't to know of the
successful Haitian Revolution and the attempts throughout America to gain freedom. Enslaved people weren't
meant to know of things like Lord Dunsmore's offer of

freedom to the enslaved who joined the British Army or accepted Spain's offer of liberty to the enslaved who reached Florida.

To avoid starvation, the majority of formerly enslaved men and women stayed in place, working for their previous owners. State legislatures across the South quickly passed the Black Codes, laws making vagrancy a crime. Freed Black men could not gather in groups of more than two people. Black people were under a curfew and initially could not vote. Mass incarceration began after the Civil War, and the penalty was often being leased to a plantation—sometimes the same one they were freed from. The Black Codes were an attempt to re-enslave the recently freed.

The Civil War effectively ended on April 9, 1865. Texas got the word on June 19, 1865 (Juneteenth). People were still legally enslaved in parts of Delaware, Kentucky, and New Jersey until the passage of the Thirteenth Amendment on December 18, 1865. Even then, there was that pesky exception allowing enslavement of prisoners, which is still used today. Freedom was a fluid concept, and free wasn't always free.

In Texas, when Major General Gordon Granger read General Order #3 on Juneteenth in Galveston, he told the newly freed to return to their plantations where they would now work for wages. He said not to show up at Army bases because the government would not support them. Across the South, many formerly enslaved people stayed in place while others wandered around with no place to go. Over a million contracted diseases or suffered

WILLIAM F.
SPIVEY

severe food shortages. 60,000 died from smallpox alone, and several thousand died from starvation. Many went to Washington, D.C., where they were herded into concentration camps. In December 1865, a group of disgruntled former Confederate soldiers in Pulaski, Tennessee, formed a social club they called the Ku Klux Klan.

What started as a bunch of ex-soldiers whining about losing not only the war but a way of life soon evolved into something much more. They became the loyal opposition to the Republican Party, which was the face of the enemy. The Republican Party was barely a decade old when the war ended, and they had already successfully elected Abraham Lincoln to the office of President. Twice. Republicans rose from the ashes of the Whig Party, and its leaders were staunch abolitionists. When Lincoln was assassinated after his second inauguration, he was replaced by strict segregationist Andrew Johnson.

The Klan quickly spread, especially after making former Confederate General Nathan Bedford Forrest their first Grand Wizard. Membership increased exponentially as did their reign of terror that included cross burnings, lynchings, and murders.

The Republican Congress got busy passing the three Reconstruction Amendments: the Thirteenth, abolishing slavery; the Fourteenth, granting most of them citizenship; and the Fifteenth, granting them the right to vote. The Klan was opposed to all of that, spurring a wave of violence that didn't go unnoticed by Congress. In 1870 and 1871, Congress passed strict anti-Klan acts that almost wiped out Klan activity in the South. The other major political party at the time was the Democratic Party. While America once enjoyed multiple political parties with a chance of winning the presidency, every president after Millard Fillmor's election in 1850 has been from either the Democratic or Republican party. The Democratic Party was aligned with states' rights, especially when it came to enslavement.

Many members of the Klan wore a badge during the day and a hood at night. Democrats (Klan members) created poll taxes and literacy tests, along with more violent methods, to curtail voting among formerly enslaved Black people. When Congress directed federal troops to go after the Klan and enforce voting rights for Black people, Reconstruction gained a stronghold.

Another critical front of the Reconstruction movement was education. White and Black churches, notably the American Missionary Association and the African Methodist Episcopal (AME) Church, were instrumental in creating learning institutions. The Freedmen's Bureau was established to help the newly freed connect with family members separated by the war. They advocated for the free men and women in courts, attempted to negotiate wages when they worked on plantations, and also established schools for those who had been denied the opportunity to learn to read and write.

The Freedmen's Bureau was initially intended to exist for a single year. When the states' resistance became clear, Congress voted to renew their charter, having to override the veto of President Johnson. His version of reconstruction focused on giving white Southerners reparations and restoring land they lost during the war. After Union General Sherman granted up to forty acres (no mule) to formerly enslaved people along the Atlantic coast in Field Order Fifteen, President Johnson restored almost all that land to its pre-war white owners, granting them the improvements made by the formerly enslaved.

Despite the existence of Black Codes, White Leagues, Red Shirts (Klan-like chapters whose members marauded in broad daylight), mass incarceration, and voter suppression, the Reconstruction Era saw many advances for the formerly enslaved. Black men gained a semblance of political power as they won statewide elections in Mississippi and Florida. Black men were elected to Congress, though being seated was sometimes problematic. Black townships formed in the South, and as Americans expanded westward, Black Americans went with them, establishing Black communities in the West.

The only reason Black progress occurred in the South was the continued presence of federal troops. These troops kept the peace when Black voting would otherwise be prevented, or Black leaders would be threatened or killed. There would have been no recourse in the courts for transgressions against Black people, though sometimes the troops themselves were the violators. Soldiers raping Black women was a common occurrence. The presence of federal troops was a thorn in the side of white Southerners who wanted their way of life returned.

Their opportunity came in 1876 during a contested presidential election. Four states, Florida, South Carolina, Oregon, and Louisiana, disputed which electors would be certified. The Democratic Party was one Electoral College vote shy of winning the Presidency, with twenty votes disputed. In an actual smoke-filled room, the Compromise of 1877 was worked out, where all twenty of the disputed votes would go to Republican Rutherford B. Hayes in return for the removal of the federal troops. Democrats sacrificed a presidency they wanted badly for what they desperately needed, the soldiers' removal.

Even before Rutherford B. Hayes took office, Ulysses S. Grant removed the troops from Florida. When Hayes took office, he removed the rest. Hayes did the South one more favor the following year, signing the Posse Comitatus Act of 1878, ensuring the troops would never return to protect the formerly enslaved people. It may be unclear when Reconstruction officially began between 1863 and 1867, but there's no question Reconstruction ended in 1877 with the removal of federal troops.

REDEMPTION

At the end of the Civil War, much of the South, including major cities like Atlanta and Richmond, was in ruins. Plantations were in shambles, and an occupying force had dismantled the political structure. Even worse, pride had been decimated, and honor was lost. To return to the Union, states had to agree to the Fourteenth Amendment and recognize the emancipation of enslaved people. Henry Louis Gates described the Redemption period as a time "when the gains of Reconstruction were systematically erased and the country witnessed the rise of a white supremacist ideology that, we might say, went rogue, an ideology that would long outlast the circumstances of its origin." Most people have heard of Reconstruction, but Redemption lurked in the background, described by different names to make it more palatable.

REDEMPTION (PART 1): ERASING THE GAINS. The withdrawal of federal troops kick-started the process of rolling back Reconstruction. The Black representatives to Congress were either forced to resign, serve out their terms and not run again, or were defeated at the ballot box, as Black voters were mostly unable to vote. Then came the enactment of Jim Crow laws and the enforcement of segregation. In the same manner as the Black Codes recreated slavery, Jim Crow did what it could to replicate the Black Codes. While the Black Codes were limited to Southern States, Jim Crow spread across the land, and segregation was established everywhere, especially in public schools.

Segregation was enforced throughout the South for public pools, hospitals, jails, drinking fountains, and residential homes for the elderly and handicapped. You may have heard of separate but equal? Segregation fostered no such thing, as facilities and institutions for Black people were always inferior. Without regard for the Fifteenth Amendment which codified the right to vote regardless of race, color, or previous condition of servitude, Black people were discouraged from voting by enforcement of special laws or threats of bodily harm.

The courts, including the United States Supreme Court, joined in dismantling the rights of Black people. Prior to 1865, the Supreme Court had only struck down Congressional Acts as unconstitutional twice. Between 1865 and 1872, however, the Court did so thirteen times, negating most of the anti-Klan acts. The Republicans who once fought for diversity, equity, and inclusion of Black people now ignored their plight. Sometimes white supremacy is defined by looking the other way when injustice occurs, as long as it doesn't happen to you.

WILLIAM F. SPIVEY

REDEMPTION (PART 2): RESTORING THE GLORY OF THE CONFEDERACY. After rolling back and discrediting the gains of Reconstruction, next came making heroes of the Southerners who allegedly fought, not to preserve slavery, but for heritage and states' rights. The Articles of Secession from each state made clear that leaving the Union was about enslavement. Virginia mentioned "the oppression of the Southern slaveholding States." Georgia discussed its "dispute with Northern states over African slavery." South Carolina describes "an increasing hostility on the part of the non-slaveholding States to the institution of slavery," specifically mentioning the refusal of other states to comply with the Fugitive Slave Act. Redemption was/is about re-establishing the deep entrenchment of slavery by another name.

Slavery is often considered America's original sin, though descendants of Native Americans might disagree. Redemption requires the erasure or rewriting of history so that America can continue to promote American

47

values and American Exceptionalism. The wrongs in history continue to be erased, as are the stories of those who overcame tremendous obstacles.

REDEMPTION (PART 3): ENSURING WE NEVER FORGET. The granddaughter I mentioned at the beginning of this chapter will spend much of the summer with my wife and me and receive unexpected history lessons. I think when she asks me questions like the one about segregation, it's

to change the subject from her performance in school and not staying on top of her homework. I don't expect her to know the terms I've mentioned, like Red Shirts, and names like Gabriel Prosser and Denmark Vesey.

We will read this chapter together and when she gets to something she doesn't know, she'll be required to research it and explain what it is. She'll pretend she understands to keep from looking it up, but I'm prepared to question her knowledge when I suspect she's faking. I encourage all readers to research as needed.

I can simplify the transition from Reconstruction to Redemption by sharing an incident in Camilla, Georgia, near her great-grandmother's home in Americus, Georgia, where her maternal grandmother was born.

By July 1868, Georgia had fulfilled the requirements of Congress's Reconstruction plan and had been readmitted to the Union. President Andrew Johnson considered Georgia's commitment met and removed the federal troops. That September, white Georgia Republicans joined with the Democrats in expelling the newly elected Black senators and Black representatives in the lower house from the General Assembly on the grounds that they were at least one-eighth Black.

Black Republicans and a few whites in Albany, Georgia, planned a march and rally in response. The march began in Albany and was to end at a Republican rally at the Camilla courthouse, twenty-five miles away. Mitchell County whites, however, were determined that no Republican rally would occur. Sheriff Mumford Poore met the marchers at the city's outskirts and asked them not to enter and to give up their guns. Unable to get the protesters to stop the march or disarm, Sheriff Poore returned to town and arranged a "posse" to greet them.

WILLIAM F. SPIVEY

According to all reports except the sheriff's, when the marchers neared the courthouse, armed white men began shooting at the protesters from positions on roofs and doorways to shops. A dozen marchers were killed, and over thirty were wounded. News of the event was sent by telegraph, and newspaper articles appeared nationwide. The Camilla Massacre is credited with suppressing Black votes in the November election. In Albany, white leaders committed fraud at the polls, deliberately misplacing many Black votes or changing them to Democratic ones. White Democrats, the racial minority in southwest Georgia, carried the election in Georgia.

Sheriff Poore gave an affidavit in which he claimed the shooting began when his friend James Johns fired a shot into the ground, as opposed to the witnesses who saw him shoot into the crowd. Freedman's Bureau sub-assistant commissioner O.H. Howard conducted what passed for an investigation. He took a few affidavits which went into a file. No one was prosecuted, and life in Camilla went on. Military rule was re-established in Georgia. Troops remained in several states until their removal became a bargaining chip to resolve the disputed 1876 presidential election with the Compromise of 1877.

Camilla was the massacre nobody openly talked about. Laws were passed in Georgia to prevent people from carrying guns to a courthouse or public gathering, but not the posse that attacked the Camilla marchers. Sheriff Poore continued serving, and no arrests were made. There was no public acknowledgment by the city of Camilla or Mitchell County that the massacre even happened until 1998. A historic marker was placed, and people returned to not talking about it.

Each civil rights movement has been accompanied by a wave of new Confederate monuments and statues and efforts to rewrite history into a kinder, gentler experience. Currently, portions of American history can no longer be taught because it might make white teachers and children feel bad. Black heroes are being erased from government websites, and books focused on race are being removed from libraries. An executive order has been issued targeting the Smithsonian National Museum of African American History and Culture, demanding that articles and displays contributed to the museum be withdrawn or dismantled.

Reconstruction lasted between ten and twelve years. But Redemption, the plan to revise history and idolize whiteness and the Confederacy, is forever.

William F. Spivey resides in Palm Coast, Florida, and has a Bachelor of Arts in Economics from Fisk University. With the help of many, he transformed from a basketball player to a historian and writer. He is the author of the historical fiction novel *Strong Beginnings* and the collection of essays *Estranged Americans: Fallacies of Freedom, Citizenship, and Racism.*

Chapter 4

Jim Crow:
The Boomerang That
Comes Back
as Fascism

By J Gray

THE END OF the American Civil War and Emancipation were two very clear steps forward for African Americans. The end of chattel slavery, recognition of Black citizenship, and the right to participate in governance as full members of the nation, brought approximately 2,000 Black men to governmental positions of power between 1866 and 1877. But these moves toward diversity, equity, and inclusion created a "blacklash"—a violent, racist lashing out against Black folks from a not insignificant portion of white society, while the other portion did little to nothing to stop it. Post Reconstruction, the emergence of domestic terrorist groups like the KKK, legislation like the "Black Codes" in southern states and Jim Crow laws took America in general, and Black people specifically, one step back.

It's a pattern we see repeated post President Lyndon Johnson signing Civil Rights legislation and again, after the election of President Barack Obama. Segments of white American society violently reacted and are presently reacting against diversity, equity, and inclusion—meaning, Black people.

NAMED FOR A blackface minstrel character, Jim Crow, this American legal system of discrimination lasted from 1877 to 1965. Keep in mind, none of this was long ago. My great-grandfather was born enslaved, the son of his "master." My grandparents lived under Jim Crow laws for the first sixty-five years of their lives. My parents lived under Jim Crow for the first thirty years of their lives, and as a sixty-one-year-old Black woman, I was born into Jim Crow. It ended when I was two years old. The recent acquisition of civil rights is the reason we don't really know each other at all.

In a white supremacist nation where difference equals disdain, separation only reinforces the differences for white Americans. It creates a fertile ground for mystery and distrust to grow. Lies, stories, and myths often revolve around intelligence, violence, tanning, hair texture, pain tolerance, or penis size. There's no end to the racist ridiculousness and depravity. To state the obvious, separation deprives Black Americans of free will, opportunity, and the pursuit of happiness. Jim Crow laws enforced social, commercial, and legal discrimination on both state and federal levels. They also mandated separation of the races in all public facilities, schools, transportation, parks, libraries, drinking fountains, restrooms, buses, trains, and restaurants.

With the lines drawn, signs emblazoned with "Whites Only" and "Colored" reinforced white supremacist ideology in both overt and covert ways. The laws created inferior living conditions, substandard wages, inferior education, and nominal protection. And, as has now become clear to previously unaware white Americans, there has never been protection for African Americans from the American police, legal, or judicial systems. Without civil rights or protections against discrimination, many doors were closed to African Americans.

Enslavement morphed into physical and mental confinement, accompanied by random daily doses of humiliation and terrorism. Life continued to be difficult and dangerous, though wrapped in a different cloth. This fear of random violence continues to be very real for Black people in the United States. My father told stories of seeing the front pages of Black newspapers with black-and-white photos of Black men hanging from trees on a weekly basis. Maintaining distance between Black and white Americans is one of the key mechanisms used to reinforce the idea of inferiority, deny the humanity of Black Americans, and gaslight the citizen soldiers of white supremacy.

Plessy v. Ferguson created the "separate but equal" doctrine in an attempt to supersede the Fourteenth Amendment and legalize racism. Enforced separation and denial of equal access makes equality impossible. This becomes more evident when one considers all the things one can't be and places one can't go. With limited opportunities, one could only dream about working in various professions. There's a reason why the first Black people to do many things in the United States are still alive and walking around: Their accomplishments didn't happen all that long ago. The domestic disease of racism continues to starve the nation of all the talent within our borders, to block all the people who'd like to contribute to making life better for human beings at home and abroad.

Even within the confines of segregation, African Americans were able to build successful communities, businesses, and towns throughout the nation. And, some of those very same financially successful Black communities became targets for racists and white supremacists like the KKK. Entire towns were burned to the ground from the 1870s to 1954, with their inhabitants massacred or run off their property. From Wyandotte, Michigan to Sheridan, Arkansas, segregation wasn't good enough for some white Americans, so the terrorism and genocide continued.

My own Black family is from Washington, D.C. My paternal grandfather was born at the turn of the twentieth century, only twenty-four years into the Jim Crow era. He had a high school education and worked as a janitor at the Pan American Union. He told stories about standing in the back of the elevator with his lunch bucket and riding with Secretary of State Dean Acheson. My grandfather listening to him talk about the important business of state in front of him, confirming to my grandfather how little he mattered.

The ability to work for the government in D.C. provided a security that helped stabilize the incomes for many of the city's Black residents. But salaries were such that my grandfather also had two side gigs. Legend has it that while delivering dry cleaning on foot, he was hit by a car, got back up on his feet, and continued on his route, emphatically stating, "I need this job!"

My grandmother was a dental hygienist and her family lived in her employer's dental office. My father slept in a closet the size of a single bed, and his parents slept on the pull-out sofa bed in the waiting room. Penny by penny and with the utmost frugality, they saved up for a house—something that's become almost impossible to do now in this society.

At the age of sixteen, seventy-four years into Jim Crow, my mom went to a basement party in D.C. at her friend's house. A neighborhood kid, upset he wasn't invited, threw a brick through the window and it hit my mother in her eye, clear on the other side of the room. She described feeling something warm running down her face as people started screaming. My great-grandfather, born enslaved, the son of his "master" but now a restaurant owner and family patriarch, rushed her to the hospital—a white hospital. He chose the white hospital because he thought they would have better equipment and procedures. He was well-to-do, worried about her sight, and thought he was doing the right thing by his little Black granddaughter.

The white nurse on duty let my mother lay in the bed all night without any form of medical attention. When the white doctor arrived for his morning shift, he asked the nurse why she hadn't called him in and she told him she didn't want to bother him. He said he could have saved her eye. The wait was responsible for her becoming blind. Or, more specifically, the racist nurse and her racism were responsible for my mother's blindness in one eye. Conscious, she'd heard their entire conversation. For many years she had horrific headaches as well. I remember her chewing Anacin like candy and crying on the kitchen floor in pain when I was a kid.

My mother's story is one of the factors that led me to only employ Black women doctors for myself. As the mother of twin boys, I can't help but think this might be why my children and I are still alive.

My father was born in 1935, fifty-eight years into Jim Crow. He said that the only white person he ever saw growing up was the iceman, the guy who sold you ice for your icebox. Jim Crow kept my Black father in his Black Washington, D.C. neighborhood and he described growing up in a vibrant, socio-economically multitiered Black community, replete with famous physicians, thinkers, jurists, musicians, and restaurateurs. The limits and dictates of segregation prevented African Americans with PhDs from teaching at colleges and universities throughout the nation, so they became faculty at my parent's magnet school, Dunbar High School. My father always believed their high school education was superior to that of most colleges in the nation.

Education was always stressed as part of the road to freedom in both my parents' families and in the Black community at large. We were taught that critical analysis, problem solving, freedom of imagination and thought will always belong to us. No one can ever take those abilities away, regardless of whatever else they strip from you. Knowledge is power. And, one of the most reliable and honorable professions to pursue within the Black community was that of teacher. The public school system provided stability in the same way that government services or the Post Office did.

Both of my parents attended college and graduate school in Washington, D.C. and both became teachers. While teaching was my mother's calling, it was not the same for my father. In retrospect, he'd tell me that teaching was the most meaningful job he ever had, but he was restless and wanted to try his hand at other things. Feeling as though he'd compromised and had been compromised in many ways, he kept dreaming about other employment paths.

JIM CROW CAME to an end with the Civil Rights Act of 1964, signed into law by President Lyndon Johnson. This Act ended legal discrimination in the United States and provided the opportunity my father had been searching for. In the late '60s, a multi-national corporation invited

African American candidates to take their employment test. One difficult test later (which is an entirely different story), he was an employee.

My father was thirty when Jim Crow ended. Having been separated by racism, inequality, and the poverty that came with Jim Crow, my father had no frame of reference for the culture and world he just joined. While the United States was his birth nation, it was as if he'd just landed in a foreign country. To be successful, he would have to learn to adapt fast, as well as deflect the slings and arrows shot at him for being an African American man in an all-white corporation.

Racist hostility aside, my father's new work environment was totally foreign as well. At a dinner meeting during his first few weeks of employment, my father's boss asked him to choose the chianti at an Italian restaurant. My father had never been to an Italian restaurant, nor eaten Italian food. That had been disallowed from 1877 to 1965. The word "chianti" might as well have meant pizza to him in that moment. He had no idea what the hell it was. Later, he bought books on wine and become a super knowledgeable connoisseur, mostly because he wasn't going to let his white counterparts shame him in any way.

For quite some time he navigated silverware and corporate dinner etiquette by allowing others to begin eating before him, so he could follow their lead. Neither had he been to an airport or flown in a plane before, so at thirty years old with colleagues, he travelled domestically and abroad. He was with his white coworkers each and every time he had a new and mind-blowing experience, but he couldn't let on it was all new. He said it was nerve-wracking. His blood pressure shot through the roof for the rest of his life and he always said that job took a good ten years off his life.

As one of the first in his corporate class, the pressure he put on himself to succeed was immense. He was the first Black person corporate American white people had ever known and worked with. He felt a responsibility to dispel the myths and lies of racism and to be a solid representative of Black folks.

He didn't want to let his people down in any way and also wanted to prime the path for others to come after him. I remember him "counseling" other Black corporate employees of that era at his multinational company, as well as in others. These folks came to our house to talk to him.

I was born in 1963, eighty-six years into Jim Crow. I'm the daughter of a "beneficiary" of the Civil Rights Act of 1964. For me, this meant that we'd live in four different states by the time I was twelve and that our family would desegregate a town in California. I grew up an African American kid alone in a diaspora. My mother and father's story is very different from mine because they lived under Jim Crow for the first thirty years of their lives. What our journeys have in common is racism—though it manifested differently.

What was clear under Jim Crow, where lines were drawn and signs clearly stated "colored" and "white," morphed into a psyop in which white Americans changed legislation, but rejected a fundamental change in behavior, all the while pretending they did. To mention the overt racism we encountered on a daily basis often set us up for scorn, with cries ranging from "chip on your shoulder" from one generation to "using the 'Black card'" in another. White Americans tried to gaslight us with their propaganda and ended up just gaslighting themselves.

And, here we are.

Racism is a boomerang that comes back as fascism.

J. Gray is an African American woman who desegregated a town as a girl. Her personal experience within
the nation and as an exchange student in northern Africa fostered her deep interest in culture, ethnicity, and
language. Watching the broadcasts of the Senate Watergate Hearings as a child introduced her to politics, and
college majors in political science and Spanish helped
cement her passions for justice.

Chapter 5

People Like Us

By Maré Silva

I HAVE NEVER dreamed about the U.S.
    As a child in northern Brazil, the United States felt
as foreign as Mars. Although I watched several American shows and listened to American music, there was
nothing that I could grasp in American culture. Not
when I stared at my dry motherland, praying it would
rain; nor when the drought was finally over and the
water from the roof collected into several bowls on the
kitchen floor. America felt fictional. It was too far from
the hours I spent commuting to school, too far from

the sound of my grandmother's sewing machine waking the house before dawn. I was never allowed to dream of going anywhere else, but it didn't mean I was satisfied. Despite my family raising me to be a survivor, I yearned to simply live.

It was something unheard of there, to leave one's home out of a whim.

Years before, my grandmother had been forced to leave the arid countryside, as the land that fed generations of her family had hardened to stone. She had no funds, no acquaintances, but still she brought each of her thirteen siblings and her parents to the city. Enslaving herself to textile factories seemed like fair trade for her family's well-being. That was our inheritance: the blessing and the burden of seeing others as an extension of our own bodies.

So, no, I never dreamed about the U.S., yet I taught myself English from old, donated books from the age of six. I read Hemingway and Dickinson and Morrison and Butler . . . and watched TV shows, amazed by the way Americans harnessed their curiosities into innovation. Very secretly, I indulged in American culture to feed my starved mind, with the certainty that such a way of living could only exist in imagination.

DARING TO DREAM

It wasn't until a teacher insisted I was fit for an Ameri can Embassy exchange program that my perspective changed. Against all odds, I was exactly what they looked for: a public-school student with strong academics and a history of well-established, successful community initiatives. In their eyes, I was a leader and had the potential to impact so many more lives than I already did with my volunteering projects. I was awarded a full-ride trip to the U.S., having barely ever left my home state.

Arriving in Washington, D.C., I could immediately see why people dreamed about this place. The exchange consisted of several trainings in social entrepreneurship, horizontal leadership, fundraising, and diplomacy over a month's time. We visited the Department of State and departed to different regions of the U.S. for fieldwork with local non-profits and cultural assimilation. I was highly encouraged to keep asking questions, to lead projects, and to suggest policies that aligned with my ideas of fairness. I had my struggles recognized, I grew confident in my potential, and I contemplated for the first time the idea of going to college. I was surrounded by a world of possibilities and couldn't wait to come back and write my future.

As soon as the trip ended, however, the COVID-19 pandemic devastated the world, leaving me stranded. I grew less and less content with the modest life that welcomed me home. Education and health were being dismantled in front of my eyes due to my country's governance, and there were few resources available for either changing the situation or growing into who I aspired to be. I wanted so eagerly to change things, to build solutions that could help people to have more accessible health.

Still, I did not dream about the U.S.; I saw it as a bridge between who I was and who I could become. This was no longer a fictional place, but a land where my hunger for knowledge could be fed. A year had passed and nothing had improved, so I decided to apply to American colleges. I told myself I was walking toward a country that rewards people like me—hardworking, inquisitive, resilient, regardless of where they come from. Even when that meant I would have to move away from the place that nurtured me for almost two decades. My family was heartbroken when the letters arrived. Two full-ride scholarships from prestigious colleges, one an Ivy League institution; it meant nothing to them. There was no pride, no celebration. The only thing they understood about the situation was that I chose to leave. I couldn't have agreed less, I was simply choosing better opportunities. It was not about values. It was not about America. It was about resources, I repeated.

I tried to soothe myself with the promises made by my new school. I was going to the most prestigious historically women's college in the United States, and I would not have to spend a dime for this amazing education. Contrary to my high school experience, there would be no four-hour commute, no resource shortages, and no side jobs to buy books. I was joining the leading hub for life sciences and politics, in a tight-knit community that would support me to thrive in clinical research and advocacy. I was a queer young Black girl from a Brazilian *favela* finally stepping into abundance.

AUTHORITARIANISM CREEPS IN

My arrival, however, was different from the one I had been promised. I stepped into a college deeply fractured by a growing conservatism. That led to an equally conservative dispersal of funding in academia, shrinking the opportunities for research and civic engagement for those who cannot afford to more freely pursue their passions. Despite the promises made, I was unable to join a research program at my own institution and had to take on several student jobs to cover my expenses for books and tuition, or housing and meals during breaks.

My academic development was deeply affected by such worries. During my first summer in the U.S., I was fortunate to have an American family welcome me at no cost, as my alma mater did not hesitate to mandate my move-out at the end of the school year, and I was unable to afford a ticket home. The weight of such bureaucratic apathy quickly vanished with the ongoing loss of liberties, one piece at a time. In my freshman year, I saw my school reject inclusive language in admissions and internal communication, excluding the identity of transgender and nonbinary students. In my sophomore year, I saw the rise of anti-Arab sentiment and antisemitism surrounding the Israeli-Palestinian conflict. Rallies and protests, as peaceful as they were, were condemned as breaking honor codes, and international students were

MARÉ SILVA

69

threatened with having their visas revoked if associated with these events. With the very recent memory of my own country being stripped of democracy, I recognized those losses not as isolated cases, but as the products of a systemic trend.

On January 8, 2023, conservative extremists attempted to storm Brazil's National Congress, echoing the events of January 6 in the United States. Brazil responded swiftly because we remember our past. In 1964, we descended into a twenty-one-year military dictatorship, marked by censorship, economic instability, torture, extradition, and the disappearance of countless individuals—citizens and non-citizens of Brazil.

We understand that authoritarianism does not arrive with a grand announcement; it creeps through the neglect of the most vulnerable and the creation of a mentality that fears disorder more than injustice. It idealizes a mythic past built on exclusion. The rise of fascist rhetoric has always been a prelude to the loss of civil freedoms. Americans have never known what a dictatorship is; thus, they may find it hard to note the progressive loss of their rights.

Nevertheless, I remained faithful to my scholastic mission and accepted all the jobs and long commutes to pursue my dreams. I had already taken the biggest challenge when I left behind everything I had known to come to this country. I needed to thrive. I was constantly tired, getting to sleep late, and waking up early, but soon enough, I became a student researcher in a prestigious cancer center, designing medical tools to save lives. I was still not paid and had to go through double the paperwork for getting work authorizations because of the National Institutes of Health (NIH) budget cuts and strict guidelines, but I felt so grateful I almost forgot how fragile my standing in this country was.

DREAMS DEFERRED?

In 2025, however, I faced the most defining moment of my university life: a massive non-tenured faculty strike, requesting resolution of unfair labor practices and a higher standard for protection against discrimination and harassment. What began as a typical mobilization, often seen in various academic institutions regardless of their funding or prestige, quickly escalated into a reflection of the current political climate.

MARÉ SILVA

The school not only showed resistance to providing better compensation and job security for its employees, but also opposed clauses aimed at preventing discrimination based on immigration status and visa history. When the school responded to the strike, it reduced the credits for courses taught by non-tenure-track faculty members. Such a decision directly impacts students like me, who would no longer have full-time status and could have both our scholarships and our visas revoked.

I was confronted again with the realization that my body was inherently political. Regardless of all the years I've paid my taxes correctly, adhered to all guidelines, adapted to American culture, and presented little to no resistance in accepting the often unfair treatment I

71

received due to my citizenship status, I was not worth sparing. Enduring condescending looks in immigrant-friendly environments and immediate rejections for job positions as soon as my status was disclosed couldn't save me. My school was very comfortable using me as collateral in the larger debate prompted by the immigration crisis. The same institution that urged me to join them as a promising talent in STEM was now the institution that would gladly disregard my safety in the name of saving a few dollars.

Once again, I had no vote in how my life would be led. This time, I was not facing a future of modesty with my family, but a future where I could be stopped in the street, put in a car, and not know if I was going to be deported immediately or kept in a detention center. I realized that, no matter how small my power is, I had to stand up for myself.

I joined the union in their strike, adhering to the guidelines as best I was able, hiding my identity and standing with my professors in the exact line where the college property ends as to avoid facing charges. On the picket line, one of my professors, an alumna, shared how embarrassed she felt that the college didn't live up to the values it preaches. She was ashamed to have her work for fair labor practices transformed into an excuse for the college to treat international students unfairly.

In that space with her, I felt safe to voice all the frustrations I had never admitted out loud before. That I regretted choosing this school because they lied about my financial aid package, and I was constantly tired of working all the legal hours to make ends meet. That I was repulsed by the derogatory discourse against minorities, as well as the new policies, which were often totally contrary to my values. That I didn't feel like a respected member of the community. That I held a grudge from when I had to get two emergency surgeries, and when I had nowhere to go they made me petition twice to stay in my dorm during recovery. That I hate that I came back to class barely fifteen days after such surgeries because I was afraid to lose my scholarship. That I resented the promises made, the extra miles I had to run, the sacrifices I've made just to not be treated as worthy of dignity.

MARÉ SILVA

With all those words barely set, a colleague near us asked, *"Why don't you just transfer?"*

THE DREAMS OF IMMIGRANTS

The question stung. Not just because it was tone-deaf, but also because it exposed how little people understand about what it means to be a migrant or an immigrant in this country. To transfer implies mobility; it assumes options. Again, I was confronted with the choice to leave. The illusion of choice is a common misconception. I have not chosen this. I chose to study in a private institution that prides itself on graduating the highest number of women who go on to earn PhDs in STEM because I wanted to be one of those women. I merely accepted that to have that, I would need to leave my family and my country behind.

Little does this colleague know, my major isn't even offered in my country. She does not know that there are only 2,000 Brazilian researchers in my field, who predominantly have achieved their degrees abroad or do not even hold a degree in this field. She does not know what it is to be robbed at gunpoint on your way to school and still be required to excel academically. She does not know about my life before college, nor does she understand the lives of my immigrant friends, some of whom haven't seen their families in years because the U.S. no longer maintains diplomatic relations with their home countries.

She cannot imagine what it is to fear that an arbitrary transgression, like a car ticket or a paperwork delay, could lead to a sudden change of legal status. She does not have to check her status on a crowded website every day or even bring along several documents every time she leaves her dorm to prove she is entitled to exist in this land. Her parents won't just be taken away despite their court dates and years of contributions to the American taxpayer system. The only constant in immigrant life is uncertainty.

She does not hear their cry. Nor does the average American. There is a world they don't see of the undocumented, the under-resourced, and the international student who has been invited to cross the ocean for opportunities, only to find themselves humiliated, silenced, and hidden. That invisibility is not an accident; it is by design. It is to the benefit of those in power that immigrants remain invisible, because our silence gives them permission to push authoritarian decisions over the lives of the people who build this country every day.

In this ignorance, the faculty strike came to an end after four weeks with no final contract. There have been suggestions that the college threatened to revoke the visa sponsorship of international professors involved in the strike. A charge for coercive statements and unlawful conduct was filed with the National Labor Relations Board, and they will follow up with mediation, which shall remain confidential. Still, there is solace.

Professors with over twenty-five years of service risked their positions on the picket line for their younger peers. Faculty allies offered extra courses to prevent deportations after the credit issue, and other moments of collective action that offered the hope I needed to continue this path. In their defiance, I remembered that while institutions may fail, individuals are the ones who carry the values and the power to achieve justice. When freedom feels out of reach, allyship can carve out spaces of survival and dignity for us to recover, resist, and luckily, thrive again. It takes courage rather than privilege to act in solidarity, and it is painfully hard to be brave in the world we live in today.

I NO LONGER see America as the promise of resources made by others. I see it as a daily exercise of the very ideals that first drew me here: defiance in the face of injustice, bravery in the pursuit of dreams, and the belief that one life, when lived with purpose, can change the world. These values I carry forward not as something borrowed, but as deeply mine.

I consider my presence in this country a revolutionary act against the hate-filled rising culture of today. Real America is about the people, immigrants, and citizens who keep this country growing powerfully every single day. The land of the free and the home of the brave is more than a symbolic last line for the anthem. It is a promise of shared freedom and the bravery to protect each other.

I used to argue with my family about my reason for coming here. But contrary to all my previous heated debates, it is, in the end, all about America.

Maré Silva is a queer Black Brazilian undergraduate at
a historically women's college, merging her passion for
science and civic engagement. From a *favela* in Brazil to
a cancer research lab in the U.S., she writes to remember,
to resist, and to build a better world with radical hope
and science.

PART III

The Arc of the Moral Universe

Chapter 6

Moral Courage and the Reconstruction Amendments

By ROY BALE "SKIP" DALTON, JR.

B ETWEEN 1865 AND 1870, in the wake of the Civil War, America took a powerful stride toward the ideal of a more perfect union. The passage of the Reconstruction Amendments—the Thirteenth, Fourteenth, and Fifteenth Amendments to the United States Constitution—transformed the nation's legal and moral history. Having successfully repelled the ethical repugnancy of enslavement on the battlefield, these refinements to the "law of the land" sought to inexorably embed into the law the lofty, yet heretofore unrealized goal that all men are created equal and endowed by their creator with certain inalienable rights.

More than legal additions, these amendments (U.S. Constitution: Amendments XIII, XIV, and XV) were moral declarations—rebukes to centuries of racial injustice; perhaps underappreciated at the time of their passage was the moral courage that would be required to achieve their enforcement against powerful tides of racism and repression.

RECONSTRUCTION AND LINCOLN'S EVOLUTION

The Civil War, fought from 1861 to 1865, resulted in the death of over 600,000 Americans and the destruction of the Southern economy that depended upon enslavement. President Abraham Lincoln initially framed the war as a means of preserving the Union, and, while opposed to enslavement on moral grounds, looked to its containment as the last best hope for preserving the Union.

The first Emancipation Proclamation issued in 1862, following a Union victory at Antietam, threatened the emancipation of enslaved people in Confederate states unless the South surrendered within a hundred days. While easy to proclaim a position of virtue, the fact is that Emancipation was as much a military strategy as a human rights undertaking. The Emancipation Proclamation of 1863 did not free all enslaved people but only those in areas where the federal government had no control, the southern states that had seceded from the Union.

Even so, it helped achieve the military objective as

by the war's end some 200,000 Black men served in the Union Army and Navy, securing victory and paving the way for the abolition of enslavement by the enactment of the Thirteenth Amendment. The Reconstruction period following the Civil War (1865–1877) was marked by an ambitious effort to rebuild the South and integrate formerly enslaved people into the political and social fabric of the nation. The Reconstruction Amendments formed the cornerstone of that effort (Foner 1988).

THE THIRTEENTH AMENDMENT (1865)
ABOLISHING ENSLAVEMENT

ROY BALE
"SKIP"
DALTON, JR.

Neither slavery nor involuntary servitude, except as a punishment for crime whereof the party shall have been duly convicted, shall exist within the United States, or any place subject to their jurisdiction.

—the Thirteenth Amendment,
ratified on December 6, 1865

It was the first explicit constitutional prohibition of enslavement, fundamentally altering the Constitution and repudiating the infamous *Dred Scott v. Sandford*, 60 U.S. 393 (1857), which held that Black people could not be citizens and that Congress had no authority to ban enslavement from a federal territory. Despite the Union victory, the abolition of enslavement was far from a *fait accompli.*

Passage of the Thirteenth Amendment would require enormous amounts of President Lincoln's political capital

83

and no small measure of moral courage from the voices for freedom.

Knowing that a lame-duck Congress would be more amenable to ratification, he personally lobbied legislators, making moral and political arguments for equality. His assassination in April 1865 cut short his vision for a compassionate Reconstruction, but his courage and commitment to racial equality helped enshrine the Thirteenth Amendment in law.

Thaddeus Stevens, a Radical Republican congressman from Pennsylvania, was a fierce advocate of racial equality. Stevens used his powerful position in Congress to help draft and push for the passage of the Thirteenth Amendment. Despite facing death threats and social ostracism, Stevens did not flinch. In a famous speech before the House, he declared that "the foundation of free government . . . must be laid on the equality of all men."

THE FOURTEENTH AMENDMENT (1868):
CITIZENSHIP AND EQUAL PROTECTION

The Fourteenth Amendment, ratified on July 9, 1868, spoke to the pressing need to define American citizenship and protect the rights of the newly freed population. Its key clauses include:

- Citizenship Clause: All persons born or naturalized in the United States are citizens.
- Privileges and Immunities Clause: No state shall make or enforce any law which shall abridge

the privileges and immunities of citizens of the
United States.

- Due Process Clause: No state may deprive any person of life, liberty, or property without due process of law.
- Equal Protection Clause: No state shall deny to any person the equal protection of the laws.

These clauses conferred citizenship on formerly enslaved people and laid the groundwork for civil rights protections for all Americans. The Fourteenth Amendment has become the most litigated part of the Constitution and the basis for landmark decisions on racial justice, abortion, same-sex marriage, and more. Put in the context of national citizenship, The Fourteenth Amendment codified the principle that the fundamental rights established in the Bill of Rights extended to the States and clarified that neither the State nor Federal governments could act to deprive their citizens of basic constitutional liberties.

While much of the litigation springing from the Fourteenth Amendment has centered on the concepts of due process and equal protection, even now, the basic principle of birthright citizenship is under scrutiny, crystallizing the historical fact that progress on the civil rights front is never linear and bulkheads once established must constantly be defended and shored up.

MORAL COURAGE IN ACTION. The enforcement of the Fourteenth Amendment required much more than

ROY BALE
"SKIP"
DALTON, JR.

action from the federal and state legislative bodies. While the South could grudgingly accept the abolition of enslavement, reordering the social and political culture was another thing entirely. Progress on this front required tremendous moral courage on the part of the judges and ordinary citizens.

Myra Bradwell was born in 1831. In 1855, her husband, James, was admitted to the Chicago Bar and went on to establish a successful law practice in Illinois. Well educated in her own right, Myra apprenticed in her husband's office, taught herself the law, and founded the publication Chicago Legal News. She was instrumental in drafting the Illinois Married Women's Property Act of 1861 and strongly supported women's suffrage rights. In 1869, on the recommendation of a federal judge from the Seventh Circuit, she applied to the Illinois Supreme Court to be admitted to the Illinois Bar. Her application was denied on the basis of her sex. She appealed to the United States Supreme Court, arguing that the refusal to admit her to the Illinois Bar violated her constitutional rights under the Fourteenth Amendment.

The Court rejected her appeal, holding that: "[T]he natural and proper timidity and delicacy which belongs to the female sex evidently unfits it for many of the occupations of civil life . . . [T]he paramount destiny and mission of women are to fulfill the noble and benign offices of wife and mother. This is the law of the Creator." *Bradwell v. Illinois*, 83 U.S. 130 (1873). While Myra lost the battle, she helped set the stage for future generations of women to win the war for the unfulfilled promise of gender equality under the Fourteenth Amendment.

One of the most striking twentieth-century examples of judicial courage came from Judge J. Waties Waring of South Carolina. A federal judge appointed by President Roosevelt, Waring initially held segregationist views but underwent a remarkable transformation.

In 1946, Isaac Woodard, a Black soldier, was on his way home to South Carolina after his honorable discharge from the United States Army, following service in World War II. After a dispute with the bus driver, Woodard was taken off the bus by a local police chief, Lynwood Shull, and beaten so mercilessly that he lost his sight in both eyes. When local authorities refused to act, President Harry S. Truman ordered a federal investigation that resulted in federal charges being brought against Shull in Judge Waring's courtroom.

ROY BALE "SKIP" DALTON, JR.

An all-white jury acquitted Chief Shull of the charges. Judge Waring, incensed by the injustice, experienced an epiphany on the subject of racial inequality and discrimination. He ordered that the custom of segregated seating by race would no longer be tolerated in the Charleston federal courthouse. He then issued rulings that challenged the racial status quo of the Jim Crow South, invoking the Fourteenth Amendment as a legal basis for equality.

In *Briggs v. Elliott*, 98 F. Supp. 529 (EDSC 1951), a case that would later be folded into *Brown v. Board of Education*, Waring issued a powerful dissent against the rationale of the Supreme Court's holding in *Plessy v. Ferguson*,

136 U.S. 537 (1896) that the Fourteenth Amendment permitted segregation of the races under the "separate but equal" doctrine. In his dissent, Waring declared that segregation in public schools was unconstitutional: "Segregation is per se inequality." His opinion was the first by a federal judge to reject the "separate but equal" doctrine of *Plessy v. Ferguson*.

This stance for racial equality was extremely unpopular in Waring's hometown of Charleston, South Carolina. As a consequence, Waring faced relentless hostility. He was ostracized from Charleston society, received death threats, and ultimately had to leave the state for his safety. Yet he stood firm in his belief that the Constitution required equal justice for all Americans.

Today, Waring is recognized as a judicial pioneer (Gergel 2019), along with Justice John Marshall Harlan, the lone dissenter in the *Plessy* case, whose interpretation of the Fourteenth Amendment helped lay the legal foundation for the Civil Rights Movement, finally acknowledged by the United States Supreme Court in *Brown v. Board of Education of Topeka* in 1954 (Kluger 2004).

THE FIFTEENTH AMENDMENT (1870): VOTING RIGHTS

The right of citizens of the United States to vote shall not be denied or abridged . . . on account of race, color, or previous condition of servitude.

—*the Fifteenth Amendment,
ratified on February 3, 1870*

The design of this amendment was to enfranchise Black men and ensure their full participation in democracy. In the years immediately following its ratification, thousands of Black men registered to vote and were elected to public office across the South—a remarkable, albeit short lived, achievement in American history.

MORAL COURAGE IN ACTION. Enforcement of the Fifteenth Amendment may have been the most dangerous undertaking of all the Reconstruction Amendments. White supremacist violence, especially from groups like the Ku Klux Klan, sought to undermine Black suffrage through terror and intimidation (Tushnet 1994). While the Constitution may have established these rights, the racists mobs set out to make sure they were never exercised.

ROY BALE "SKIP" DALTON, JR.

John R. Lynch, born into enslavement, became one of the first Black members of Congress from Mississippi. In his memoir, *The Facts of Reconstruction*, Lynch recounted threats against his life and the lives of other Black leaders. Violence and intimidation to suppress the Black vote was widespread and highly effective (Lynch 1913). It was helped along by poll taxes, literacy tests, Grandfather clauses, white primaries, gerrymandering, and voter registration restrictions, all designed to make sure the constitutional promise of voting rights was never realized.

Decades later, the courage of individuals like Fannie Lou Hamer—a sharecropper from Mississippi who became a national voice for voting rights—would reignite the fight. In 1964, she gave a searing speech before the Democratic National Convention, describing the brutality she suffered for attempting to register to vote. Her bravery helped pave the way for the *Voting Rights Act* of 1965, a modern echo of the Fifteenth Amendment nearly one-hundred years in the making.

THE BETRAYAL OF RECONSTRUCTION

MORAL COURAGE
AND THE
RECONSTRUCTION
AMENDMENTS

Despite, or perhaps because of, their transformative potential, the Reconstruction Amendments were betrayed in the decades that followed. With the end of Reconstruction in 1877, Southern states enacted Jim Crow laws that systematically disenfranchised Black voters, segregated public spaces, and institutionalized racial inequality.

This long period of American racial apartheid was embraced and emboldened by the Supreme Court in cases like *Plessy v. Ferguson*, upholding these discriminatory, segregationist regimes and effectively nullifying much of the Reconstruction legacy. The rise and fall of Jim Crow is the story of strong men and women of color, who in the face of unending terror, achieved the triumph of equality. Black success and the use of political power is what enraged the white supremacists (Simkins 1944).

President Andrew Johnson was not supportive of Black emancipation. The election of Grant provided hope, but federal intervention was not enough. The culture of Jim Crow in the segregated South effectively snuffed out the hope engendered by the Reconstruction Amendments. The quest to realize freedom inspired "Pap"

Singleton, the self-styled "Moses of the Colored People," to lead a group of over twenty thousand formerly enslaved men, women, and children to Kansas to escape the racism of the former Confederacy. These pilgrims became known as the "Exodusters." This exodus was also motivated by the passage of the Homestead Act of 1862, which provided 160 acres of federal land in the West to anyone who agreed to farm it. But while many Black people left the South, many more remained to fight injustice and press the cause for freedom.

Ida B. Wells, born into enslavement in 1862, was an iconic figure of moral courage (Painter 1976). Her investigative journalism exposed the lynchings used to terrorize Black people. As a founder of the National Association for the Advancement of Colored People (NAACP) and a Black female activist, she suffered death threats and public disapproval. In 2020, she was posthumously honored with a Pulitzer Prize for "her outstanding and courageous reporting on the horrific and vicious violence against African-Americans during the era of lynching" (Pulitzer 2020).

It took almost a century—through the Civil Rights Movement—to begin reclaiming the promises made in the Thirteenth, Fourteenth, and Fifteenth Amendments.

ROY BALE "SKIP" DALTON, JR.

CONTINUED RELEVANCE TODAY

The Reconstruction Amendments are not relics; they are living parts of our constitutional DNA, continually reinterpreted and reasserted in new contexts.

1. MASS INCARCERATION AND THE THIRTEENTH AMEND-MENT. The "punishment clause" in the Thirteenth Amendment has been criticized for enabling modern systems of forced prison labor. Michelle Alexander's book *The New Jim Crow* argues that mass incarceration is a continuation of racial subjugation under a new guise (Alexander 2010). Activists have called for reforms that would close this loophole and realign the criminal justice system with the amendment's original spirit.

2. EQUAL PROTECTION AND LGBTQIA+ RIGHTS. In *Obergefell v. Hodges*, 576 U.S. 644 (2015), the Supreme Court ruled that bans on same-sex marriage violated the Fourteenth Amendment's Equal Protection Clause. Justice Anthony Kennedy wrote, "The fundamental right to marry is guaranteed . . . to same-sex couples by both the Due Process Clause and the Equal Protection Clause."

3. VOTING RIGHTS IN THE TWENTY-FIRST CENTURY. The Fifteenth Amendment faces new tests today. The Supreme Court decision in *Shelby County v. Holder*, 570 U.S. 529 (2013) struck down a key part of the Voting Rights Act, leading to a wave of voter suppression laws. States have enacted voter ID laws, reduced polling places, and purged voter rolls—disproportionately affecting minority communities. The battle for voting rights is ongoing, as seen in recent federal efforts to pass the *John R. Lewis Voting Rights Advancement Act.*

The holding in *Shelby County* that Section 5 of the Voting Rights Act requiring certain former southern states to obtain preclearance of legislation that might infringe the rights of certain voters is unconstitutional and violates the states' rights to regulate elections amply demonstrates the fact that hard-fought gains in voting rights equality cannot be taken for granted. While the moral arc of the universe may bend toward justice, its path is a tortured one.

CONCLUSION

ROY BALE
"SKIP"
DALTON, JR.

The Reconstruction Amendments represent a constitutional revolution—an effort to create a more just and inclusive republic after the sin of enslavement. Their passage and enforcement demanded not only legal strategy but immense moral courage from individuals across generations: from Thaddeus Stevens to Myra Bradwell and Fannie Lou Hamer, from John R. Lynch to Judge Waties Waring.

Today, the promises of the Thirteenth, Fourteenth, and Fifteenth Amendments are not yet fully realized. But their presence in our Constitution serves as a moral and legal beacon—a call to conscience and action. They remind us that the work of building a more perfect union is ongoing, and that justice requires both bold law and brave people willing to defend it.

93

Alexander, Michelle. *The New Jim Crow: Mass Incarceration in the Age of Colorblindness.* The New Press, 2010.

Foner, Eric. *Reconstruction: America's Unfinished Revolution, 1863–1877.* Harper & Row, 1988.

Gergel, Richard. *Unexampled Courage, The Blinding of Sgt. Isaac Woodard and the Awakening of President Harry S. Truman and Judge J. Waties Waring*, Sara Chricton Books, 2019

Hamer, Fannie Lou. "Speech at the 1964 Democratic National Convention."

Kluger, Richard. *Simple Justice: The History of Brown v. Board of Education and Black America's Struggle for Equality.* Alfred A. Knopf, 1976.

Lynch, John R. *The Facts of Reconstruction.* The Neale Publishing Company, 1913.

Painter, Nell, *Exodus: Black Migration to Kansas After Reconstruction*, Knopf, 1976

Simkins, Francis B. *Pitchfork Ben Tillman: South Carolinian.* Louisiana State University Press, 1944.

Supreme Court Decisions: *Plessy v. Ferguson*, 163 U.S. 537 (1896), *Brown v. Board of Education* (1954), *Shelby County v. Holder* (2013), *Obergefell v. Hodges* (2015).

Tushnet, Mark. *Making Civil Rights Law: Thurgood Marshall and the Supreme Court, 1936–1961.* Oxford University Press, 1994.

U.S. Constitution: Amendments XIII, XIV, and XV.

Judge Dalton was born in Jacksonville, Florida, and received his undergraduate and law degrees from the University of Florida in 1974 and 1976, respectively. Nominated by President Obama to the United States District Court in January of 2011, he currently presides in the Orlando division of the Middle District of Florida.

ROY BALE "SKIP" DALTON, JR.

Chapter 7

The Second Reconstruction

By MARK DOROSIN

THE THREE CRITICAL CIVIL RIGHTS LAWS OF THE 1960S

A SERIES OF SUPREME Court decisions in the late nineteenth and early twentieth centuries constitutionally legitimized racial segregation in America and disenfranchised Black voters. In the wake of those rulings, civil rights activists and community leaders began a strategic and deliberate legal, political, and grassroots advocacy campaign to reclaim the promise of justice and equality of the Reconstruction Amendments. While this struggle was waged on many fronts, access to education became the primary focus of the challenge to Jim Crow, in large part because of the critical role education plays in accessing other fundamental rights, including economic freedom and political power.

THE SECOND
RECONSTRUCTION

Although it represented the culmination of decades of a coordinated litigation challenging segregation, the decision in *Brown v. Board of Education of Topeka* reversing the "separate but equal" doctrine for public schools is considered the beginning of the "Second Reconstruction"—a new era of expanded civil rights legislation and advocacy and that reinvigorated the prospect for meaningful equality for African Americans. Despite the promise of *Brown*, it took another ten years and a massive grassroots movement that exposed the depth and violence of American racism before Congress adopted the Civil Rights Act of 1964.

The Civil Rights Act was the first meaningful legislative action on racial justice since 1875. That law, and the subsequent Voting Rights Act and Fair Housing Act—and the judicial decisions affirming their constitutionality—fundamentally changed the nature of race relations in America. Like its predecessor, the Second Reconstruction challenged the institutionalization of white supremacy and racial oppression that infected every aspect of American life. In so doing, it helped the nation begin to close the gap between the rhetoric and reality of its promise of equal justice under the law.

THE CIVIL RIGHTS ACT (1964)

The expanding civil rights movement of the early 1960s and the increasingly violent and widely publicized responses from southern sheriffs, police departments, racist hate groups, and public mobs forced President Kennedy in February 1963 to send Congress a civil rights bill. The president was worried about losing the support of Southern Democrats however, and as a result, his initial proposal did not include the desegregation of public facilities and only imposed equal employment requirements on government contractors. Kennedy's assassination later that year, along with the growing intensity of civil rights protests and the corresponding violence in reaction, ultimately led to the passage of a much more powerful law.

MARK
DOROSIN

Congressional leaders and President Lyndon Johnson understood that bipartisan support was key to passing the civil rights bill. Southern Democratic Senators used their seniority, leadership positions, and numerous parliamentary maneuvers to keep the bill from coming to the floor for a vote. This included a filibuster lasting seventy-five days. A cloture vote to break the filibuster—which required the support of sixty-seven senators—finally passed in June. It was only the sixth time in American history that a vote to cut off debate in the Senate succeeded.

The Civil Rights Act was sweeping in scope. Its provisions outlawed discrimination in public accommodations (Title II), education (Title IV), the expenditure of federal funds (Title VI), and employment (Title VII). During congressional debates, Title II—which prohibited segregation in any place open to the public (including restaurants, hotels, parks, and transportation facilities)— was expected to produce the most virulent public resistance. It was, in fact, the first section of the Civil Rights Act to be challenged in court.

The charge that the government could not regulate private conduct was summarily rejected by the Supreme Court, which noted that the law was grounded not only in the Equal Protection Clause of the Fourteenth Amendment, but also in the government's broad powers to regulate interstate commerce. Following that ruling, resistance to the integration of public places rapidly faded. As Harvard Law Professor Randall Kennedy noted, unlike segregation in schools or workplaces, segregation in public accommodations was primarily confined to the South, and the presence of Black people in those venues was not perceived as threatening to white privilege as was racial inclusion in other areas of society.

Title VI of the Act had a far more substantial impact, prohibiting discrimination in any programs or activities receiving federal funds. As President Kennedy explained when the Act was introduced, "Simple justice requires that public funds, to which all taxpayers of all races contribute, not be spent in any fashion which encourages, entrenches, subsidizes or results in racial discrimination." Given that the federal government funded a broad range of state and local government programs, Title VI created a tool to challenge discrimination in housing, transportation, land use planning and zoning, environmental regulation, education, and health care.

Most importantly, as government decision-makers learned to avoid overt racist statements or conduct in adopting policies and practices whose racially disparate outcomes were foreseeable (like the placement of hazardous waste facilities or other unwanted land uses in minority communities), Title VI allowed individuals to challenge the discriminatory effects of government actions. This was particularly crucial, as the Supreme Court limited direct enforcement of the Fourteenth Amendment to intentional discrimination only.

MARK
DOROSIN

Title VII addressed employment, seeking to eliminate discrimination in hiring, firing, promotion, pay, and the general "terms and conditions" of employment in any business with fifteen or more workers. It also prohibited retaliation against employees for challenging discrimination, and created and empowered the Equal Employment Opportunity Commission (EEOC) to investigate and bring legal challenges against employment discrimination.

While Title VII seemed initially focused on overt and intentional discrimination, the Supreme Court's 1971 decision in *Griggs v. Duke Power* substantially expanded the power of the Act and recognized that despite its adoption, the entrenched impacts of Jim Crow could undercut its ability to remedy race discrimination. Prior to the passage of the Civil Rights Act, Duke Power policies expressly limited Black workers to the lowest positions in its plants. When the new law took effect, the company announced the "desegregation" of its workforce and abandoned its explicitly discriminatory policies. Duke then adopted generic employment testing and educational requirements that perfectly maintained the existing racial hierarchy of its workplaces.

Black workers, represented by Julius Chambers and the NAACP Legal Defense and Education Fund, claimed that the new employment policies allowed the company to lock its prior patterns of discrimination in place, thereby maintaining institutionalized inequities even in the absence of the former overtly racialized policies.

Duke insisted that any consideration of its actions or history prior to the adoption of Title VII was improper, since its admittedly discriminatory employment practices were not illegal at that time. Since those practices ended when the Act was passed, the company argued that its conduct could only be judged from that point forward, and that any consideration of its pre-Act conduct could not be considered. Title VII required that Duke stop discriminating based on race, and the company asserted that it had fully complied.

The Supreme Court disagreed. Its unanimous decision recognized that employment practices and procedures "neutral on their face, and even neutral in terms of intent, cannot be maintained if they operate to "freeze" the status quo of prior discriminatory employment practices." The Court also found that "good intent or the absence of discriminatory intent does not redeem employment procedures . . . that operate as 'built-in headwinds' for minority groups." What mattered, the Court concluded, were the racial consequences of the challenged practices, not their motivation.

The opinion was a forceful endorsement of an expansive vision of civil rights, and one that was vital if the law was to reach the practices that created and maintained institutional discrimination. The Court's holding recognized the subtle but no less malignant forms of race discrimination that continued to plague People of Color, even as more blatant discriminatory actions became illegal (and over time, socially unacceptable). Most impor- MARK
tantly, the *Griggs* decision recognized that acknowledging DOROSIN
the context and continuing effects of our history of intentional racial discrimination is necessary to fully remedy existing inequities. As Justice Harry Blackmun explained a few years later, "In order to get beyond racism, we must first take account of race."

THE VOTING RIGHTS ACT (1965)

As noted above, the Civil Rights Act of 1964 primarily addressed the use of government funds, education, employment, and public accommodations. It took another year, the powerful testimony of Fannie Lou Hamer at the 1964 Democratic convention about how she and others were beaten by Mississippi police for trying to register to vote, and the "Bloody Sunday" march in Selma to push Congress to pass the Voting Rights Act (VRA).

The VRA was a groundbreaking measure designed to eliminate existing practices used to prevent Black people from voting, as well as prevent the implementation of new voter suppression tactics. Section 2 prohibited any measure that denied or restricted the right to vote on the basis of race, ending the use of literary tests and other barriers to registration. Section 2 also covered redistricting and other procedural changes to elections that could dilute Black voting strength, like switching from districts to at-large elections.

The other key provisions of the VRA were Sections 4 and 5, which targeted states and localities with the worst history of voter suppression. If a jurisdiction met the criteria of Section 4, it would then be subject to the "preclearance" provisions of Section 5. This meant that any proposed voting changes in those jurisdictions had to be submitted to the Department of Justice or a federal court for a determination that those changes would not adversely impact the rights of Black voters before going into effect. At the time the VRA was adopted, Section 4 applied to six states in their entirety (Alabama, Georgia, Mississippi, South Carolina, Virginia, and Louisiana) as well as almost half the counties in another (North Carolina).

The VRA had an immediate impact, especially on the registration of Black voters. Between 1965 and 1967, Black voter registration went from nineteen percent to fifty-three percent in Alabama and from seven percent to sixty percent in Mississippi. By 1980, the percentage of Black voters registered in the South surpassed the rest of the country. And the changes in voter demographics led to new Black political representation. In 1968, Virginia, Florida, and North Carolina each elected the first

Black member of their respective state houses since Reconstruction. By the mid-1980s, there were more Black elected officials in the South than in the rest of the nation combined.

In 1980, a ruling from the Supreme Court substantially narrowed the scope of the VRA and the ability of voters to bring claims of discrimination. Congress moved quickly to amend the act to override the decision and restore the full scope and power of the landmark civil rights law. The VRA was reauthorized in 1982 for an additional twenty-five years, and then again in 2006, both times by overwhelming margins.

MARK
DOROSIN

THE FAIR HOUSING ACT (1968)

The Fair Housing Act (FHA) was the final major civil rights law of the Second Reconstruction. While the Act had been debated for years, it took the assassination of Rev. Dr. Martin Luther King Jr. and the protests that followed to finally push the Congress to move forward. While some earlier Supreme Court cases addressed aspects of housing discrimination (in one case, to protect the rights of a white homeowner to sell his property to a Black family, over the objections of his white neighbors), the entrenched intentional residential segregation of Black families impacted every aspect of their lives, including access to education, job opportunities, safe and healthy neighborhoods, basic public services, and the power to build wealth through home ownership.

The FHA was designed to address the range of discriminatory conduct that produced those racially disparate impacts and to have a broader scope than simply eliminating housing discrimination. Senator Walter Mondale, the law's sponsor, stated that the purpose of the Act was to create "truly integrated and balanced living patterns." The FHA itself is explicit on this point, demanding the Department of Housing and Urban Development (HUD) "administer programs and activities related to housing . . . in a manner affirmatively to further the policies of [the FHA]." That is, not merely to end segregative policies and practices, but to actively promote residential racial integration.

The Supreme Court emphasized this critical component of the FHA in one of its earliest rulings on the law, when it held that white tenants in a building that excluded Black residents had the right to sue under the FHA because the law guaranteed all people the right to live in an integrated community. Other cases recognized that even though housing segregation in America was arguably the result of government policies and practices implemented without any overt or express racial animus, the FHA reached the discriminatory impacts of those policies and practices. These included exclusionary land use and zoning decisions, denial of development permits, attempts to concentrate or prohibit low-income or multi-family housing, and a range of other purportedly "race neutral" government actions that prevented meaningful racial integration.

EXTRAORDINARY VICTORIES, TOO SHORT ENJOYED

The Second Reconstruction began with the fearless and radical grassroots activism and incredible persona. sacrifices of thousands of Black Americans demanding racial justice. In the face of legal and extra-legal violence (including death), and against what seemed like a corrupt and intractable legal system, those dedicated people demanded that our nation live up to its promises of justice and equality. And beginning in the 1950s, their efforts began to bend the moral arc of the universe.

MARK DOROSIN

Their refusal to compromise eventually moved the federal government to pass comprehensive legislation to remedy the toxic effects of race discrimination that infected every aspect of American life. The Supreme Court, perhaps atoning for its role in providing legal sanction to two centuries of white supremacy, expanded and enhanced the impact of the legislation. It seemed, as Sam Cooke prophesized, "a change is gonna come."

But like its nineteenth century forerunner, the Second Reconstruction soon faced a coordinated and aggressive backlash. Conservative, anti-civil rights advocates committed to rolling back the progress of racial justice found sympathetic allies in Supreme Court justices appointed by Nixon, Reagan, and G. W. Bush. The progress made toward remedying America's legacy of discrimination was recharacterized as "special treatment" for People of Color at the expense of white people.

The Supreme Court has severely limited the scope of the Civil Rights Act and worked to eliminate the ability to legally challenge the racially discriminatory impacts of government decisions and practices. More recently, the Court eviscerated the Voting Rights Act and determined that efforts to address the continuing legacy of racial injustice in America actually constitute illegal discrimination against white people. At the same time, state and local governments are determined to prohibit schools and businesses from discussing racial inclusion, even as the nation grows more racially and ethnically diverse every year.

It's time for the Third Reconstruction.

Mark Dorosin is an Associate Professor of Law and the Director of Legal Clinics and Field Placements at the Florida A&M University College of Law. He has been a civil rights lawyer and litigator for thirty years, working to address the continuing impacts of racial segregation and exclusion in housing, employment discrimination, environmental justice, restrictions on political participation, and racial disparities in education.

Chapter 8

Memory, Migration, and the Making of Home

By Consuelo G. Flores

"When a foreigner
resides among you in your land,
do not mistreat them.
The foreigner residing among you
must be treated as your native-born.
Love them as yourself,
for you were foreigners in Egypt.
I am the Lord your God."

—LEVITICUS 19:33-34 (NIV)

WHEN MY PARENTS crossed the border, there was no social media to document what they experienced as immigrants. Now, we see the immigrant experience—both good and bad—through the eyes of each person who has a smart phone and documents their respective lives for posterity or to memorialize what's happening in the moment.

I have many friends who've done this, not just for themselves, but for those immigrants whose lives have been disrupted, dislocated, and sometimes, destroyed because of these documented raids by Immigration and Customs Enforcement (ICE) agents. While I've not witnessed these occurrences, as we've come to know, social media and the internet brings us face to face with realities we used to just hear about, occurrences we may have wanted to ignore. For example . . .

A couple of weeks ago, a friend posted a video. She was driving past a Mexican restaurant, one that my husband, who is white, and I have frequented. Their food is good, and I've never felt insecure while dining there—until now. Now, I feel like I'll need to carry my birth certificate with me if I dine there again, which I doubt I will for the foreseeable future. Why? Because my friend posted a video on social media of ICE agents entering the restaurant and a few minutes later, showing a stream of people (servers, busboys, dishwashers, cooks, and customers), their hands zip-tied behind their backs, being led to waiting vans.

None of these people were criminals. None was engaged in nefarious activities. They were all in a restaurant either working or dining. And they were all Latine. The video of this raid shook me to my core. Many of the people who were taken looked like my parents, my siblings, like me, like my children.

No one knew where they were going to be taken or what was going to happen to them. Not their families or even they themselves.

The events with ICE have left me disturbed and in disbelief. How can ICE agents and government workers effectively change overnight? Is it that easy to go from CONSUELO G. FLORES helping to harming vulnerable people? I wondered about my own family, how was it that they—we—escaped from this miscarriage of justice.

In 1958, my family left Ejutla, Jalisco, Mexico for the land of opportunity—the United States of America. With the freedoms born from the Declaration of Independence, the Constitution, and the Bill of Rights, the discouraged, oppressed, and political prisoners from every part of the world courageously made their way to these shores seeking a new life and new freedoms in a new land. This hope brought many families to this country. My family was one.

My father came first as part of the Bracero Program. This program started because of World War II when men were going into the military and the crops in the United States were left unattended. The U.S. needed men to pick crops that were rotting either on the vine or in the fields. The U.S. contracted men from Mexico to come and do this labor-intensive work. As a Bracero, my father would go wherever the crops needed harvesting. He traveled along with hundreds of other men on trains throughout the United States.

When the war was over and the American men came back home, the United States ended the Bracero Program but many of the Mexican men who could stay did so. My father decided to stay and, instead of working the fields, found work at a slaughterhouse, processing both pork and beef products for public consumption. He later secured his green card, then brought our family to the U.S., which included my mother and eight brothers and sisters. They entered the U.S. legally after months of waiting for their green cards in the town of Tijuana, Mexico.

My family settled in East Los Angeles, where a sister and I were born. Once in the U.S., our house became a waiting station in the Mexican immigrant underground railroad. It was always full of people coming and going from Mexico to the U.S. and back again, in search of the American dream my family had apparently found. Our home was a beacon of Mexican culture, radiating like a Roman Catholic candle. Jesus hung on different sized crosses throughout the house. He was shedding a tear on a black velvet painting in the living room and illuminated by the burning wick of a veladora in the dining room. There were statues of Mary on the mantle above our fake fireplace, on the nightstand by my mother's bed, and on a corner shelf on the kitchen wall above the stove overlooking every pot of beans my mother cooked. Then there were statues of Saint Jude, patron saint of the desperate, keeping a vigilant eye on us from the dresser in our bedroom and on the tank above the toilet in the bathroom. Whatever we were doing, we became comfortable being watched.

Although salaries were much better in the U.S. than in Mexico, we were still in need of many things. Of course there were bills to pay, food to provide, and shoes, clothing, medicine, the daily cost of living . . . for a family of twelve. I was lucky. I was too young to work.

To have enough money, my father and eight older brothers and sisters would go to Bakersfield to pick onions during the harvest. I remember they would all pile into the old Chevrolet and leave early in the morning. It would be dark when they left and dark when they returned. They would be dirty, hungry, tired and smelling of sweat and onions. They'd shower, eat, and go to sleep to rest up for the next day.

During the harvest, they would work every weekend unless the car broke down, but then, we would be short of money. It was hard labor, and the youngest working was eight years old, not much of a childhood. My family worked hard, with honesty and dignity and always respecting the letter of the law. It was a difficult life, but it was our life and everything seemed okay. But then the Vietnam War happened.

Even though my brother Luis was not born in the United States, he was drafted and went to war as a soldier. He fought for this country, the one that had given his family such a grand opportunity. What we didn't know at the time was that the military was sending Black and Brown soldiers to the front lines in disproportionate numbers. More Black and Brown soldiers were coming

CONSUELO G.
FLORES

115

home wounded or in body bags than their white counterparts, despite there being more white soldiers.

At home, my older brothers were being targeted by the Sheriff's Department in East LA as well as the LA Police Department. This peaked during the protest against the Vietnam War that spiraled into a "riot" when the Sheriff's Department attacked demonstrators at what was then known as Laguna Park. During this chaotic time, *LA Times* journalist Ruben Salazar was killed by a sheriff while sitting at a bar waiting for an informant who was supposed to share inside information with him about police brutality in the East LA Sheriff's Department.

These events made my parents question whether immigrating to the U.S. had been the right thing to do. Their son was fighting a war and being sent to the front lines first; their sons at home in LA were being targeted by authorities. Ruben Salazar, the voice of our community, was murdered by the Sheriff's Department. Meanwhile the girls in our family were being directed to take home economics instead of being guided toward higher education.

At that time, my parents decided that we would return to Mexico as soon as we had enough money. That statement, which I heard repeatedly as a child, along with the persecution I felt our community continued to face, made me feel unsettled and in limbo. I felt like I couldn't hold on to any type of friendship or relationship or desire to have a future in this country because my parents continued to say that we were going to return home to Mexico. Neither the U.S. nor LA was going to be home.

Eventually the talk of returning to Mexico waned. Following my brothers' lead, I pursued higher education and went to college. As a child of immigrants, it was not a given that I would attend a university, but I did. Earning two degrees in this country, I like to say that I claimed my education.

After my college years, I began teaching young adults about Mexican culture, including art, literature, music, and some of the most popular celebrations. I was shocked when some of the students refused to participate in these lessons because they associated the content with "wetbacks." I asked them why they felt that way when they came from the same background. They refused to accept this truth. While I prohibited them from using epithets, they continued to do so outside of class.

Unlike my family's experiences, immigrants today face greater, sometimes violent challenges as they navigate this new country. Despite the disdain those young students had for immigrants, today there is more vitriol lobbed against foreigners. And like those students, sometimes the hatred and violence come from their own U.S.-born community members, who ironically are susceptible to those same attacks because they often share the same skin color or features.

As a consequence of the current state of our country, most immigrants, especially those who come from countries with Black or Brown populations, are not

CONSUELO G.
FLORES

117

welcome. This country no longer embraces the freedom once touted here. Instead, immigrants have somehow come to represent the idea that they're "taking" something away from "Americans," when the reality is, if it weren't for immigrants, Americans wouldn't have much of the food that we enjoy. Immigrants are the human resources who, like my family did, pick and process much of the food we eat.

There are many other contributions immigrants make to this country. The Greater Southern California area is one of the best examples of how significant the contributions of immigrants have been. Our SoCal community represents over a hundred countries with cultural pockets throughout LA and Orange counties. Aside from the Mexican American community in East Los Angeles, you can find Little Central America (which includes Guatemala, El Salvador, Nicaragua, Costa Rica, and Honduras), Little Tokyo, Koreatown, Chinatown, Little Armenia, Little Ethiopia, Little Bangladesh, Historic Filipinotown, Thai Town, Tehrangeles (Persian Square), Russian-speaking Jewish community in West Hollywood, and in San Pedro, Via Italia and Croatian Place. Orange County includes various Asian ethnoburbs in cities like Anaheim, Buena Park, Costa Mesa, Garden Grove, and Westminster that include Vietnam, Korea, India, and Taiwan. These areas give us a tapestry of experiences, foods, customs, and the opportunity to interface with others who are different from us. This leads to the prospect of a better understanding of each other.

The current administration has wrongfully identified People of Color as potential criminals sometimes for just having a tattoo. Regardless of whether they were seeking asylum in this country, they've been deported without due process and often not even to their country of origin. Now, there's been an uptick in immigrants from countries with a predominantly white population. The major difference is that many times, People of Color are seeking asylum from persecution, wars, or even gang strife in their homeland. If we look at our foreign policies with the countries from where asylum seekers originate, we can often find a correlation between U.S. interference in their government and the rise in those seeking sanctuary in our country. Regardless of the reasons they come, we should welcome people from all countries.

CONSUELO G. FLORES

To welcome them, the U.S. needs effective policy changes when it comes to immigration. We need to treat our foreign brothers and sisters in a humane manner. There needs to be more judges hearing the cases for those who seek refuge. There needs to be more immigration offices and personnel to process applications.

In the meantime, everyday citizens can support immigrant communities and contribute to a more informed conversation. We can have town halls or community gatherings where we can share each other's experiences, have small break-out groups to give members an opportunity to truly connect.

The Church helped my family when my parents and eight brothers and sisters first came to the U S. The congregation collected food and clothing as gifts. The community welcomed us, learned about us, and embraced us. We can do the same for today's immigrants. We can visit communities outside of our own and ask questions. We won't learn about each other until we start to dismantle our own biases, address our own fears of "the other," and reach out to one another. The reality is that unless you are an indigenous person, a member of the First Peoples of the land that we know as the United States, or a descendant of Africans who were kidnapped, brought to this country by force, then enslaved, we are all immigrants.

I recently attended a family funeral with all but two of my living siblings. After the funeral, I met Rachel, my eldest sister; Lupe, my eldest sister-in-law; and my eldest brother Ramón at our parents' graveside. We came to visit them and our brother, whose ashes were buried with our mother. I played with my grandbabies and listened as Rachel and Lupe talked about life. We were atop a hill that overlooked the Los Angeles skyline. At that moment when the sun dipped behind the buildings and the city seemed to glow, Rachel asked Lupe, "Can you believe how far we've come? From the dirt-poor town in Ejutla to this beautiful place in this grand city." We all took a deep breath and without missing a beat, Lupe pulled out a rosary. "Would you like to join me in prayer to give thanks to our parents for bringing us here?" she asked. We all bowed our heads and prayed. Indeed, we had all come through a long, challenging, fruitful, and amazing journey.

I wish the same for today's immigrants.

Consuelo G. Flores is a respected artist, educator, and cultural practitioner specializing in Day of the Dead altars. She has curated exhibitions, led academic workshops nationwide, and directed both short and full-length plays. A published poet and active member of a literary collective, she has also produced cultural programming at Grand Performances and curated exhibitions at Avenue 50 Studio.

ABOUT CONSUELO G. FLORES

PART IV

Repealing the 20th Century

Chapter 9

Fascism: American Style

By MICHAEL GREINER, PhD, JD

A MERICAN POLITICS HAS become incredibly polarized. Some have argued that the last time Americans were so divided we became embroiled in a civil war. Those of us on the left often accuse the conservatives of being "Nazis" or "fascists." Oftentimes, such language does more to obscure the argument rather than to clarify it, especially given the fact that most people have trouble defining those terms. That realization begs the question: What exactly do "Nazi" and "fascist" mean?

Both "Nazi" and "fascist" are emotionally charged terms, generating strong reactions. In short, they refer to a political movement that we will call "fascism," since Naziism can really be understood as a specific example of this political movement that came to power in Germany in the 1930s.

Historically, the term "fascism" dates back to post-World War I Italy. The Fascist party was a political movement most closely associated with Benito Mussolini, the

dictator who led Italy into an alliance with Germany in World War II. Interestingly, the German National Socialist party, or the Nazis, ultimately headed by Adolf Hitler, at least in part modeled themselves after the Italian political movement even though the Germans became the most prominent advocates of this ideology. In 1932, before Hitler came to power in Germany, Mussolini and Giovanni Gentile described their ideology in a political essay, "The Doctrine of Fascism."

Other fascist-like movements in Europe to emerge during that period include the Spanish Nationalists, who, under the leadership of Francisco Franco, won the Spanish Civil War; the Party of National Unity in Hungary; and the Iron Guard in Romania. Similar movements arose in the Netherlands, France, Greece, and even Brazil. In fact, the Peronist political movement headed by Juan and Eva Peron after World War II in Argentina was deeply influenced by Italian fascism.

Political scientists have struggled to define fascism, since it tends to vary from country to country. That said, there appear to be a few consistent characteristics. In his book, *The Anatomy of Fascism*, Columbia University historian Robert O. Paxton argued that ultranationalism, combined with the myth of national rebirth, is a key foundation of fascism, believing that "the chosen people have been weakened by political parties, social classes, unassimilable minorities, spoiled rentiers, and rationalist thinkers." In short, fascism argues for a return to a time when the country was "great," before it was supposedly weakened by people who are not members of society's dominant group. In Italy, Mussolini promised a return to the greatness of Rome, while in Germany, Hitler looked to a mythical "Aryan" past.

MICHAEL GREINER, PHD, JD

This assumption leads to several essential attributes of Naziism and fascism:

1. The movement must advocate for the rights of a group it sees as the "rightful" heirs of the nation, such as ethnic Europeans.
2. The movement seeks to protect these "rightful" heirs from certain groups that threaten their dominance, such as Jews, immigrants, and LGBTQIA+ individuals.
3. The movement targets those members of the dominant group who betray it with their openness to these marginalized groups. Such individuals often include members of the political left and intellectuals.
4. The movement will advocate an aggressive foreign policy aimed at prioritizing the national interest and returning the nation to its historic greatness.
5. To achieve these aims, the movement will curry favor with elites through a capitalist economic policy

in which the government aggressively involves itself in generating economic growth by prioritizing the wealthy.

6. Finally, the movement will support the elevation of a strong leader, empowered to accomplish these goals and overcome any opposition by any means, even force if necessary. In essence, an autocrat.

After World War I, and especially once the Great Depression began in the early 1930s, Europe was fertile ground for such a political movement. Every country involved in the war, even the winners, was devastated by its impact. France, who won the war, suffered one and a half million soldiers killed in action, at least 18 percent of those who served, leading to a demographic crisis there. The economic catastrophe that Germany endured after the war, with its sky-high inflation, is well documented. Such crises led to people looking for answers, and fascism provided clear, simple answers that came with catastrophic consequences.

One would think that such a political philosophy would be anathema in the United States, with its Constitution and Bill of Rights. Unfortunately, many elements of fascism have appeared in American history before. In particular, the period after the Civil War generated a reaction among white Southerners that presaged European fascism. During the period known as "Jim Crow," anti-Black movements seized control of several state governments after the federal government stopped enforcing laws passed to protect the formerly enslaved.

In essence, Jim Crow promised a return to a period of greatness in the American South: the period when enslavement flourished prior to the Civil War. White Southerners, bitter over their loss in the Civil War, resented the political and economic power that was afforded Black Americans as a result of federal enforcement in the period of Reconstruction. The southern economy was also hobbled by the loss of free (stolen) labor in the form of enslaved people.

As a result, a political movement emerged in the former Confederacy in which white people sought to take control of their state back from Black people and their northern allies, known as "carpetbaggers" because of the luggage they used when they moved to the South. These states passed laws aimed at denying Black people political power and education, forcing them back into a state of servitude.

MICHAEL GREINER, PHD, JD

To support this political movement, white Southerners developed a mythology known as the "lost cause." Advocates of this ideology, such as the Daughters of the American Revolution, erected memorials across the South celebrating Confederate military leaders, and propagated a narrative in which victorious Union general and President Ulysses S. Grant was a corrupt drunk, and Confederate general Robert E. Lee was a hero. The movement purported that the cause of the Civil War was not enslavement, but was instead a fight for freedom against a tyrannical federal government, or "state's rights"

Like fascism, then, Jim Crow advocated a return to a mythical period of greatness that was only taken away

129

from society's dominant groups by extending rights to society's marginalized. To impose this regime on the former Confederacy, its supporters engaged in a state-sanctioned reign of terror, openly attacking Black people and their allies without legal consequences to intimidate them into compliance.

White people were lynched as well as Black people during this period. In fact, in the period just after Reconstruction ended, from 1882 until 1885, lynchings of white people far outnumbered those of Black people. This explicit violence was paired with social and economic pressure for white people to support the racist regime. This fact leads us to our final characteristic of fascism: the requirement of its potential opponents to refrain from fighting it out of fear.

Many, including former President John F. Kennedy, used the apocryphal saying misattributed to Edmund Burke, "the only thing necessary for the triumph of evil is for good men to do nothing." The rise of fascism in its various forms provides an example for this sentiment. Although it frames itself as a majoritarian philosophy, protecting the rights of the nation's true heirs, often the group it advocates for does not in fact constitute a majority of society.

For example, in Iraq, Saddam Hussein led a fascist-like government that sought to privilege Sunni Muslims, even though they represent only about 40 percent of the Muslim population in that country. Similarly, the Nazis never held majority control of the German Bundestag (legislature).

In the United States, non-Hispanic white people will become a minority of Americans within the next fifteen to twenty years. Arguably, this changing demographic is part of the reason a segment of white people has become so reactionary of late when it comes to immigration and citizenship: They fear their loss of privileged status as they will no longer constitute a majority of Americans.

In America, we have been quickly moving from a white majority to a multi-ethnic population. According to the Pew Research Center, the decade from 2010 until 2020 is the first time that the number of people Americans who identify as "white" declined in real numbers, not just as a percentage. During that time period, the white population declined by 5.1 million people while the overall U.S. population increased by 22.7 million.

MICHAEL GREINER, PHD, JD

As a result, the U.S. Census Bureau estimates that the percentage of Americans who identify as "white, not Hispanic or Latino" now rests at just 58.4 percent, a number that topped 80 percent in 1980. This trend, which has been accelerating over the past few years, means that white people will represent a minority of the American population by 2045.

To try to retain their privilege, even with their declining numbers, white people have had to engage in a variety of strategies. After all, not all white people agree with the idea that America becoming a multi-ethnic democracy is a problem. When white people made up 80 percent of the population, a certain percentage of that group could support granting rights to traditionally oppressed groups without endangering the white power structure. However, when white people represent only 58 percent of the population, as they do now, or an even smaller group, as they will in the future, they can ill afford such defections without losing power.

As a result, fascist supporters rely on tactics ranging from bullying up to and including physical violence to compel acquiescence of those who do not agree with their priorities. Such efforts can only succeed if fascism's opponents allow themselves to be intimidated. Without such implicit consent, there is no way for a fascist movement to impose the control it seeks over government.

This reality indicates what opponents of fascism need to do: organize. We need to make it clear to everyone that multi-ethnic democracy is not a threat; instead it is an opportunity that will help raise all boats. America need not be a zero-sum game. Instead, opportunity and freedom can increase for everyone. How we get this message across, however, is the topic for the rest of this book.

Michael Greiner, PhD, JD, has managed political campaigns across the country, worked on Capitol Hill, and served as Deputy Mayor of Warren, Michigan's third largest city. His firm, specializing bankruptcy law, has helped thousands of families and businesses restructure their debts. And his research has been published in *The Harvard Business Review, The Journal of Business Strategy, The Journal of Business Research,* and other top journals.

Chapter 10

The Impact of Dismantling Government Agencies

By LECIA MICHELLE

A S GOVERNMENT AGENCIES are gouged and federal workers fired, we see the consequences of these reckless changes. Unless you're one of the wealthiest Americans, these changes will directly affect you. The question is which changes, and how much. Everyone will feel the effects at different levels, but most of us will feel further financial pressures as safety nets on which we depend are fractured or removed. Let's talk about some of the changes and how they might change people's lives.

It took nothing more than a threat for companies and universities to cave and renege on their commitment to DEI. Diversity, equity, and inclusion initiatives don't create an unfair advantage for anyone. It's a way of recognizing and valuing what makes us unique and embracing those differences. When leaders aren't willing to fight to retain this part of their organizations, it means that DEI is just a statement with no real meaning behind it.

What many fail to understand is that, when governments punish us for trying to provide pathways for marginalized people to have a chance at more opportunities, what they're saying is they don't want everyone to have the same opportunities. They don't value differences. They don't care about being inclusive. They have no interest in anything equitable or fair. The people demanding that DEI practices be dismantled fully understand that a diverse workplace increases their bottom line. So consider for a moment what that means: They hate the idea of marginalized people receiving any help so much that they're willing to lose money over it.

DEI initiatives, while they strive to create opportunities, are similar to trying to stop a leak in a dam by merely putting your finger into the hole. We need far more aggressive measures to stop the practices that make DEI a necessary initiative. There are no laws that require any organization to actually commit to those three words. So they can slap a slogan on their website without any real intention of following through with what they're saying. When threatened with lawsuits or the withholding of funds, many companies will return to business as usual as they remove DEI language from their websites, recruitment literature, and training modules. And it only took the click of a button for it all to go away.

Once it's gone, it's easy to give the same tired excuses as to why very few people from underrepresented groups work in these organizations and why the ones who do only stay for a short time before they leave. It's easy to blame them instead of the toxic work culture. "They weren't a good fit." "They just couldn't handle the work." "They weren't qualified to do the job." If entities never dig any deeper, this is the narrative that will allow them to feel no responsibility for creating such an uninviting, trauma-inducing workplace that these people were forced to leave.

DEVALUING EDUCATION

What about the systems in place that make DEI necessary? We only have to look at the state of public education to understand how underrepresented groups are set up for failure. According to the National Center for Education Statistics, the graduation rate for public schools in 2021-2022 was eighty-seven percent. Sounds great, right? Not so fast. Graduation rates are vastly different in wealthy suburbs versus urban areas. And it's easy to blame the children attending these schools. "They're not working hard enough." "They don't care about their education." But none of that is true.

The United States still remains, in many ways, a segregated country. And our school districts tell the story. If you visit a public school in a wealthy suburb of Chicago, then visit a school in south Chicago, you will witness the stark differences in amenities. Students attending schools in the poorer areas face an uphill battle to receive a good education, let alone go on to college. So keep that in mind as we face the dismantling of the Department of Education. Who will suffer the most? We already know the answer. Without any oversight, Black and Brown students will fall even further behind. And it's by design. Keep marginalized people ignorant and those in charge can control their ability to fight back.

GLOBAL HEALTH CUTS

As more departments are dismantled, the people they've tried to help are further exposed. For example, defunding research monies hits universities particularly hard. Consequently, people in medical trials or who have serious diseases will suffer. That's because vital research is done at the academic level. And if funds like National Institutes of Health (NIH) grants cease to exist, that means the robust research that universities conduct has to be scaled back or, in some cases, even stopped.

So consider what that means.

Not only does it affect research that can save lives, it also hinders collaboration amongst academics. These collaborations and partnerships are essential in the medical and scientific fields. These partnerships can occur globally, where people from all over the world work together with the goal of trying to create treatments for our deadliest illnesses and diseases. And these researchers depend on the agencies that assist them with this work.

Now that the United States is no longer a member of the World Health Organization (WHO), our leaders won't even know when a pandemic is happening. Without advanced warning, there's little time to respond. That puts us all at risk. We only need to remember the results of COVID to know the consequences of not taking these situations seriously.

Historically, the United States has been instrumental in driving global health policies and initiatives through its membership in WHO. Without that, our country will no longer be a part of decisions that affect every citizen of the world. Instead, we're left with leaders who would rather deny that our country needs help from anyone to ensure our own citizens remain healthy. Without WHO, we're running blind with no direction. We'll have no idea what's coming and no plan to fight it. The outcome could have deadly, long-lasting effects. Traditionally, the United States has also helped respond to health crises around the world. Without our help, other countries will face challenges when addressing their own health emergencies.

Our reckless withdrawal from WHO creates a domino effect that reverberates around the world. Along with WHO, the freezes to U.S. Agency for International Development (USAID) also have deadly consequences. These monies provide humanitarian aid to people who depend on that help for their very survival. Consider some of the deadliest natural disasters and what happens if aid is no

LECIA MICHELLE

longer available. Some other programs funded by this agency include AIDS epidemic control, mine clearing in Asia, and war relief in the Ukraine. It seems as if these decisions are focused on abandoning our most vulnerable citizens to figure out solutions on their own. But without this money, any solutions will be out of their reach. And people will die.

DOMESTIC DISASTERS MADE WORSE

Closer to home, what are the consequences if help is unavailable in our own country? As the planet continues to warm, we're seeing unprecedented natural disasters devastating our communities. Yet the leader of the Federal Emergency Management Agency (FEMA) has been fired, thus thrusting the country into a time of uncertainty as to who will help communities when these disasters inevitably occur.

Consider what could happen when another wildfire, tornado, hurricane, or flood destroys a community and the government agency we depend on to provide assistance is no longer able to do so in a timely and coordinated fashion. People will die. And the ones who survive will have no place to go. Throwing FEMA into chaos means that, during a community's time of need, they may have no one to depend on but themselves. So as people are trying to make sense of losing everything, they might be left on their own to figure out how to get basic necessities such as medical care and housing.

Recently, St. Louis, Missouri, was hit with an EF3 tornado, which means winds reached up to 165 mph. As of the writing of this article, almost two weeks have passed and FEMA is nowhere to be found. As in most natural disasters that hit a community, the people most at risk are the ones struggling to make ends meet. It's no different in this situation. The people of North St. Louis took the brunt of the destruction. Their older homes were no match for the tornado, and now many of them are homeless. As local officials try to help, the absence of FEMA can be both seen and felt. Driving through the impoverished neighborhoods in this area, you now see rubble where once families lived, worked, and survived.

LECIA MICHELLE

Travel mere minutes from this neighborhood and you'll see pristine streets lined with towering mansions and perfectly manicured lawns. What you'll also see are trucks and workers clearing debris and tarping roofs. These homes are newer, so none of them were destroyed. And unlike North St. Louis, people were insured and can afford to repair the damage. If you're wondering why people don't insure their homes, it's an easy answer. If you're already struggling to feed your family, you'll forego insurance to make sure no one starves. It's a game of roulette that no one wants to play. And none of us could have foreseen that a hurricane would hit the heart of the city.

Regardless, without federal assistance, the residents of North St. Louis may never be able to come home. Where does that leave them? Many residents of the area had lived in their homes for generations. Some of these homes were over one hundred years old. Run down? Perhaps. But no one can say that the homes weren't loved. My maternal grandparents lived in North St. Louis, and I remember visiting them as a child. The neighborhood was, and still is, decidedly working class. People are trying to keep a roof over their heads, and many are one step away from homelessness. Without their homes, that is now a reality.

REJECTING THE MELTING POT

As the dismantling of federal agencies continues, we can expect these disruptions to have consequences that will reverberate for generations. Some of the most obvious changes, while immediately affecting one group, will change all our lives for the worse. Immigration has been a talking point for many people in this country. They have convinced themselves that somehow hardworking immigrants who come here are taking American jobs. Yet the people who work here, if they are here illegally, contribute to this country's bottom line. They pay taxes. Many work jobs that most Americans can't imagine doing and for considerably less than minimum wage, which we know isn't even enough to support a single person let alone an entire family.

Our universities welcome students from other countries who want to come here for an education or to conduct research in areas that could have a positive impact on everyone's lives. We're seeing these same people

142

arrested with the intention of deporting them. In some cases, these are academics that are on the cutting edge of medical research. Or they're experts in cyber security. Or they're simply someone's spouse who is trying to achieve the American dream. And so-called patriots have decided that they no longer belong here, even if they're here legally.

But these are Americans.

I would even argue that they are more American than the ones demanding they leave. Immigrants still believe that America holds the key to achieving their dreams. It's the place where these dreams can come true if you're willing to work hard. What we're finding out is that no one is safe. First, the people who aren't born here are targeted for deportation. Who's next? Although I was born here, as a descendant of enslaved Africans, I don't know the origins of my ancestors. Does that mean I'll be deported too?

Every American hurts if any one segment of us is targeted. The people who consider themselves part of the population holding power understand that. We must be clear about something. The wealthiest in this country make up the ruling class. The rest of us do not. Let that sit with you for a second.

You might think that, because you're not in a marginalized group, you're safe. But no one is. For example, the recent tariffs imposed will make imports more expensive. What most people don't understand is that businesses don't pay those higher taxes. Consumers do. Yes, we as purchasers of those goods will now pay more for them.

LECIA MICHELLE

143

Love your morning cup of coffee? Congratulations. Coffee will now cost you more. And it wasn't cheap to begin with. While there are local coffee growers, the bulk of coffee is imported from other countries.

Clothing? The same thing. Most of our clothing is made outside the U.S. With tariffs, Americans will pay more for clothing. And who will that affect most? If I had to hazard a guess, I would say working- and middle-class families who are trying to provide for their children.

In addition to clothing, let's think about what else kids need when they're in school. Notebooks? Pens? Pencils? You guessed it. They will also cost more. So families who were struggling before will struggle even harder. Many consumer goods we take for granted simply will cost us more money. Why? Because the wealthiest Americans refuse to care about anyone else other than themselves. While we won't see shortages of necessities like we did during the COVID pandemic, we will have to dig deeper into our pockets to purchase those necessities.

A RESURGENCE OF CONTAGIOUS DISEASES

Speaking of COVID, I'm sure we remember how the virus made its rounds in our schools. Children and teachers died. Yet we still have a vocal population of Americans who don't believe in vaccinations, even when their own children die from a preventable illness. When workers are fired and the ones now leading agencies responsible for health-related decisions share the dangerous beliefs

144

that vaccinations don't work, it opens up the country to outbreaks of illnesses we haven't seen in decades.

I'm flabbergasted that in the year 2025, we're seeing a resurgence of measles in the United States. And the response is the opposite of what it should be. Because of federal funding cuts, clinics that normally would be dispensing vaccinations are instead shutting their doors. This leaves many children unprotected from this potentially deadly and highly contagious illness. Which brings me back to our schools. We know how easily colds spread amongst children. However, colds aren't usually deadly. When a child contracts measles, they can develop complications such as pneumonia. And yes, they also can die.

Some anti-vaxxers believe that holding a measles party where all the children can just get the illness and develop immunity is the answer. But think about it for a second. The only thing participants are doing is actively spreading an illness that will infect more than just the people at this event. Consider the other at-risk people in the community who could die from measles. Our older populations and people who are already immunocompromised face an even higher risk of complications if they contract measles.

Instead of believing the horror stories from people who have no idea how vaccines work, let's educate ourselves. We must teach ourselves about the important history of vaccinations and how they have prevented countless epidemics in our country. Then we must demand that the government make them readily available so that we give Americans the best chance at prevention and recovery.

WITH THESE RECKLESS changes to federal agencies, Americans will have a harder time simply living their lives. As grocery prices increase, health care suffers, and education continues to slide, we will see dire consequences of these dangerous decisions. The only people who will be immune to these consequences are this country's elite. They don't have to worry about the price of eggs, losing their jobs, or receiving a good education. As we scramble to figure out a new normal, their lives will go on as if nothing is happening.

The majority of us have no point of reference for this level of privilege and wealth, and we never will. So we need to wake up as Americans and understand that we're on our own. That's why our votes and our voices must send a resounding message that we've had enough.

Lecia Michelle is the author of *The White Allies Hand-book: 4 Weeks to Join the Racial Justice Fight for Black Women*. She has led racial justice groups and conducted training on allyship. As a Black woman, Lecia Michelle understands the importance of fighting for and protecting our most marginalized communities.

Chapter 11

The Land of the Free and the Home of the Brave

By STEVE DRAGSWOLF

"Consequently Indians have come to believe that their problems were soluble by conformity to white culture (if there is one). Now that Indian people have realized that their problems are legal and not cultural, legal solutions will be found through political action, and Indian people will not only be free to revitalize old customs, but also to experiment with new social forms."

—VINE DELORIA JR., *CUSTER DIED FOR YOUR SINS*

IN THE FOURTH grade, my teacher, Mrs. Pacheco, had all of us sing a song as she walked between us and placed each student in categories based on how we sang: soprano, alto, tenor, etc. She divided us up once more into relevant sections and had us sing another song. As she wandered between us while we sang, she would whisper in the ears of some students and skip over others. She passed me by and, when she was done, she had a selection of the best voices in the class that were set to sing the main parts of songs she had prepared for an evening pageant celebrating the uniqueness of America performed by various elementary classes.

As we continued to practice in the days leading up to the event, she pulled me aside one day and told me I'd be joining the ranks of the best voices to sing two special songs: "The Star-Spangled Banner" and "This Land Is Your Land."

"I'm not choosing you because you sang well," she told me. "I'm choosing you because you're a Native American." In her mind, she felt forced to include me. How could she compose a group of kids singing about America and not have the proper diversity represented for such storied songs as the ones we were singing?

When the night of the event came, every student was dressed up. I wore a button-up shirt, a sweater vest, and baggy black slacks that I hoped covered my noticeably white sneakers. We gathered in a small section near the stage to prepare. Each student was given some sort of accessory to signify a particular race of people. I received a large multicolored construction paper feather attached to a brown construction paper headband that I dutifully placed on my head. We took the stage where I was stiff and insecure as the others sang loudly and confidently. I stood distinctly with the great singers in the class, looking like an Indigenous Alfalfa from *The Little Rascals*, with a stubborn feather sticking straight up from the back of my head.

We sang these songs, or, as in my case, mumbled through them, with care. Our first song concluded with the popular refrain, "O'er the land of the free and the home of the brave." We ended the event with another popular refrain, "This land was made for you and me." We sang these songs in a combination pizza restaurant and arcade, a popular place for birthday parties, called Pistol Pete's. The restaurant's mascot, a dual pistol wielding cowboy, evoked the imagery of the many cowboy and Indian battles of the Southwest. We sang these songs in the land of celebrated Spanish conquistadores who ravaged the Indians of New Mexico and had bronze statues honoring them in the city. We sang these whitewashed homilies of the American religion like our lives depended on them.

STEVE
DRAGSWOLF

THIS LAND WAS MADE FOR YOU AND ME

Many people still speak today about Indians in the past tense and as a singular group with no variation. There is no monolithic pan-Indian, yet western students primarily learn about Indians as such in history, anthropology, or archaeology classes. Rarely do we view Indians in modern terms and rarely as individual nations. Recent pop culture events, like the success of the FX TV show, *Reservation Dogs*, have helped re-introduce Indigenous people and culture to a local and even global audience, reminding people that, yes, American Indians are still alive, and, yes, Natives are very modern.

Yet, the popular Indian myth is still largely relegated to historical references in mainstream thought and belief, referring to Indians mostly in the past tense and possibly considered extinct. However, Indians from the more than 570 federally recognized tribal nations, and Indians from the many tribes continuing their fight for federal recognition, are still here arguing for tribal sovereignty and demanding the ability to live as freely as they once did in these lands known as the United States of America.

Woody Guthrie's song, "This Land Is Your Land," was a sarcastic critical statement against the great American philosophies of capitalism and property rights, but the song has since been neutered to enforce American colonial greatness. Instead of questioning John Locke's philosophy of property that our American founders latched on to, children sing this song as though we each have parcels of land to occupy in this abundant nation, furthering the American myth of exceptionalism and individuality over everything else. Land ownership is an American ideal; a proper citizen should own land and develop it. But how did U.S. ownership of land develop?

Indian relations during the initial years of U.S. colonist settlement served to categorize tribal groups as distinct nations that could help or hinder the birth of this nation. Intergovernmental treaties were established between various Native nations with sovereign entities like Britain and the fledgling American colonists striving to set up their own country. The goal of these first treaties was either to make peace with or at least confirm Native neutrality for a particular side during the Revolutionary War and other skirmishes.

STEVE
DRAGSWOLF

Over the subsequent years, treaty-making continued between tribal nations and the U.S. government with the official establishment of the Bureau of Indian Affairs (BIA) in 1824, which sought to oversee Indian relations but instead was the primary catalyst for abuses toward Indigenous people in this country.

These later treaties focused on providing special determinations for tribes as sovereign nations, defined land rights and boundaries for these tribes, and offered resources such as provisions and health care in exchange for land earmarked for colonist settlements. The U.S. continued to grow and enact treaties with sovereign tribal nations to procure land for itself.

The resulting goal was meant to provide for shared land usage between these sovereign nations, securing independence and peace in a land made for you and me. However, as colonialism often goes, the sins of greed and corruption spread, resulting in empire building instead of relationship building.

On November 3, 1972, over 500 American Indians entered the BIA office in Washington D.C. and declared it was now a "Native American Embassy." Angered by centuries of abusive assimilation policies, defined as attempts by the U.S. government to make Indians purely citizens of the United States by destroying citizenship in tribal nations, Indigenous activists of the sixties and seventies began taking direct action against the American government and its continuation of colonialism.

American Indian Movement (AIM) activists filled the halls of the BIA's federal headquarters, declaring it Indian land and threatening to take over other buildings held by the United States Department of the Interior, which to this day oversees America's Indigenous peoples along with wildlife, natural resources, federal lands, and forests. The underlying picture we derive by such a department overseeing Indians is that the government still sees and treats Natives as wild elements of nature to be tamed through dominion.

But by declaring the BIA federal building a "Native American Embassy," AIM was loudly stating that Indians are sovereign citizens of nations whom the U.S. government signed treaties with and should instead be engaged through the U.S. State Department, which manages international affairs between sovereign nations.

A few years before the 1972 occupation of the BIA offices in D.C., Indian activists occupied the abandoned Alcatraz Federal Penitentiary hovering in the middle

154

of a channel off San Francisco. This abandoned federal land, the occupants argued, was now Indian land due to the century-old Treaty of Fort Laramie between the U.S. government and the Sioux tribe which stated any abandoned, unused federal land would be returned to the Indigenous people that once occupied that area.

Over 500 treaties have been made between the U.S. government and sovereign tribal nations throughout our history. Yet, every single treaty was either broken, amended, or nullified to allow for colonist overreach in the "new land." These Native activists threw the American government's wanton dismissal of treaties back in its face.

STEVE DRAGSWOLF

The occupation of Alcatraz Island ended after nineteen months, but not before Indian activists offered to settle things by selling Alcatraz back to the U.S. government for its initial price of forty-seven cents an acre. Indians also offered to buy the land with twenty-four dollars in beads and red cloth, the supposed transaction that led to the purchase of Manhattan Island. Both offers were declined. Imperialism does not appreciate sarcasm, it seems.

ASSIMILATION AND TERMINATION POLICIES

In the decades leading up to these actions, the BIA was engaged in assimilation policies as well as tumultuous attempts at equally harmful termination policies, defined as attempts to get rid of Indian land and special federal determinations for tribes (i.e., treaty rights) by dismantling Indian nations altogether.

During the termination era, which extended through Eisenhower and Kennedy's presidencies, though the latter did tone down those policies, Indian termination was justified with the goal of decreasing fiscal responsibility. As a result, the government started the process of ramrodding the termination of tribal nations as quickly as possible.

It started with attempting to remove all tribes in California, Florida, New York, and Texas along with individual tribes in Montana, Oregon, Wisconsin, Kansas, Nebraska, and North Dakota. After spending time experimenting with the ins-and-outs of removing tribal lands, the government realized while attempting in the late fifties and early sixties to terminate the Menominee in Wisconsin that they saved far less than initially thought and instead incurred millions in costs to bring tribal roads, schools, and health care up-to-par with the general public.

Remember that the U.S. government initially established treaties exchanging resources like roads, schools, and health care for land used by American states. The government has always been reluctant to meet the requirements of treaties its forebears made with Indians.

These termination policies also helped to drive American Indians off the reservation and into large cities where they would naturally acclimate and assimilate. 71 percent of Indians today live in cities instead of their tribal lands, effectively making tribal self-determination more difficult through its loss of people due to the

rising trend of Urban Indians. In all, over a hundred
tribes were terminated.

THE UNIQUENESS OF THE INDIAN FIGHT

The Indian struggle has always been a legal battle to retain tribal sovereignty on Indian land that has led to
small squabbles between Indian activism and the struggles of other marginalized groups.

One particular slight on American Indigenous activism was the refusal by many Indian activists to join in the
Civil Rights Movement led by the Rev. Dr. Martin Luther
King Jr. As the fight continued for equality under the
law for Black people, and by extension all people, many
Indians ultimately refrained from participating largely
because they believed joining the fight for equality that
Dr. King advocated for would further justify assimilation and termination policies for Native Americans in
the mind of federal officials.

STEVE
DRAGSWOLF

If the government saw that Indians were fighting
to be equal with white people, then assimilation and
termination would be proven true. However, American Indians were never fighting to be equal with white
people in America; Indigenous people were fighting for
sovereignty and self-determination on their own land.

Vine Deloria Jr., in his book, *Custer Died for Your
Sins*, recounts that Indian activists in the 1950s and
1960s consistently received pushback for their reluc-
tance and refusal to join in these marches in the Civil
Rights Movement. But, as an early Civil Rights Act was

signed by Eisenhower, that same administration was also engaged in Indian termination, a fight Natives bore on their own.

While many American Indians today are thankfully involved in activism to better the lives of marginalized people across America, the Indian fight remains tightly focused on tribal sovereignty, and it's an issue largely ignored by others due to its unique stratifications. Urban Indians are culturally assimilated into greater American culture but not legally assimilated, and as a result many Indians today misunderstand the extraordinariness of our fight.

For Indians, some of the best activists are always going to be lawyers who can effectively fight for recognition of tribal sovereignty in the courts, especially with the Supreme Court. Law, it seems, is the language of the colonizer, and Indians need to speak it fluently.

WORRY FOR FUTURE INDIAN RELATIONS

American Indians have since enjoyed better relations with the BIA and other governmental powers with the occasional roadblock here and there, typically brokered by the sometimes Swiss-cheese like and contradictory determination of Indian rights by the Supreme Court. Despite these changes, the stance of the federal government has never reached consensus on allowing Native nations their full sovereignty as initially established through the existing 500+ treaties, and based on its actions, still prefers assimilation.

In times like these, with federal programs being cut and departments being defunded, the many Native nations in America wouldn't be terribly sad if the BIA or other federal departments overseeing Indigenous affairs were defunded if it meant full tribal sovereignty would be restored to Native nations, freeing Indians from centuries of abuse and paternalistic oversight and safeguarding them from future abuses.

The issue we face, though, is that the removal of those programs by an administration set on an "America First" mandate could be the precursor of the total removal of Indian lands that have been fought for and protected for centuries, leading to the abolition of self-determination and self-government for Indigenous people on their ancestral lands, a right that supersedes the establishment of the U.S. Constitution.

STEVE DRAGSWOLF

Instead of federal oversight, a "Native American Embassy" is necessary because, whether either side likes it or not, the U.S. and Native nations are inextricably tied together due to treaties and land rights. This country succeeded in part due to the treaties that helped establish greater boundaries for settlement on this land and there were many promises made for how the U.S. was going to pay for these lands, all held in treaty.

THE LAND OF THE FREE AND THE HOME OF THE BRAVE

As a child, I sang the "Star-Spangled Banner" at Pistol Pete's with the smell of pizza in the air and sounds of arcade games in the distance. I was the loudest and most confident when singing "O'er the land of the free and the home of the brave," mostly because it's all I remembered. However, my confidence in that statement remains today.

As an American Indian from the Mandan, Hidatsa, and Arikara Nation (federally recognized as the Three Affiliated Tribes), I often struggle to see how America fully lives up to its ideals as the land of the free. Seeing the continued destruction of tribal sovereignty rights by both Republican and Democratic administrations, and by their Supreme Court appointees, has soured my opinion on America's definition of freedom.

Yet, as an American Indian, I still love America despite these problems. I, like all other American Indians, am a dual citizen of this country and my own tribal nation, and I want to see both succeed. Indians have fought against a government that sought our destruction for centuries. The U.S. government went from outright violence to subdued annihilation through destructive applications of law that still tear away our treaty rights today.

While we still have a way to go to be the land of the free for all people, I know for a fact we are still the home of the brave due to the many people in this country who stand up to powerful men and women with truth, passion, and the hope that we will someday experience freedom for all, void of oppressive policies, draconian governmental actions, and violent retribution.

As for us Indians, and as it has been for centuries, our mere existence will continue to be our resistance.

Steve Dragswolf is a writer from the Mandan, Hidatsa, and Arikara Nation. He currently lives in Albuquerque, New Mexico, and is interested and invested in Indigenous people, Christianity, and storytelling, often intermixing the three. Read more of his work at BadLodge.ccm.

Chapter 12

Jesus's Rejection of Christian Nationalism

By DREW DOWNS

"When Jesus realized that they were about to come and take him by force to make him king, he withdrew again to the mountain by himself."

—JOHN 6:15 (NRSVUE)

I HAVE AN EARLY memory from the balcony at the back of our church. I was probably four or five, sitting in the dark wooden pews with my mom and sister, peering over *The Book of Common Prayer* I was reading like a novel. My mom tapped me on the shoulder and whispered in my ear, "This is the one prayer we want you to memorize," and I listened. *Our Father, who art in heaven . . .* These are the opening words to the most famous Christian prayer, often called The Lord's Prayer. In the Gospels, Jesus says this prayer is how his followers are to pray when they pray, which sounds like a solid reason to keep praying this way. The prayer itself focuses on these things: hallowing God, spreading the justice of God, the equal distribution of food to all who are hungry, the forgiveness of all debts, protection from evil, and the reign of God over earthly authority. This makes it a surprising prayer for those people of faith who don't seem all that interested in equity, justice, and forgiveness. Which, these days, seems like a lot of them.

Jesus's prayer offered his disciples an alternative vision from the one they knew and took for natural: a world dominated by kings and conquering empires, and in which religious leaders were complicit in carrying out the ambitions of the empire. A vision which eschewed personal gain for common support, and places forgiveness above retaliation, indebtedness, and other means of domination and control. In short, the Lord's Prayer is anti-supremacy.

As a Christian, I've given up being surprised by the actions of many of Jesus's faithful followers which seem to utterly reject the teachings of Jesus. It is not surprising to catch wind of yet another Christian claiming a love for Jesus and the AR-15 they won at a church raffle. We have come to expect racism and anti-immigrant rhetoric from people living in a nation founded by immigrants on stolen land, and following a religion based on welcoming immigrants and refugees.

This hypocrisy is by design. Since the 1960s, a politically conservative and active part of the evangelical movement, led by wealthy families with fortunes made from beer and newspapers, sought to dominate and control American Christianity. First by funding alternative schools and think tanks, then by orchestrating the takeover of major denominations—notably succeeding in transforming the Southern Baptist Convention in 1983 and failing to take over The Episcopal Church—though their support of a schism in the latter severely weakened the denomination in the 2000s.

Through a robust, orchestrated effort to cast a singular Christian vision through absolute control of the courts, Congress, state houses, schools, and the law itself, this part of the evangelical movement is trying to define the right way of being Christian while erasing the inherent diversity within Christianity and our shared culture. In its place, we are offered an ugly, abusive religion that hardly resembles the Christian faith at all.

This aberration of Christianity seeks out control only to beget violence and champion cruelty. Like the enslavers who strained the Bible for credibility to own other humans, eugenicists and today's supremacists find that every path to power leads through rejecting the very humanity of God's children. Note that their endeavor is not about intellectual consistency—it is purely an attempt to attain and maintain control.

It is infuriating to see this happen in real time. As I write this, the Rev. Dr. William Barber II was arrested for praying in the U.S. Capitol at the same moment today's supremacists touted religious freedom at the White House with a prayer circle. Let us focus on the way these two events represent a stark contrast in our perception of what faith is. Rev. Barber was praying for justice while the president was praying for power.

It may be tempting to unwittingly accept the evangelical frame itself—that they fully represent Christianity—thereby erasing the prophetic witness of other parts of faithful Christianity. This, too, has represented the popular response to the rise of evangelicalism, a movement with roots in the Reformation, but in the modern mind is synonymous with conservative, and now, through political domination and journalistic neglect, has become synonymous with Christian. This is how we find ourselves reading about the conservative desire to protect a Christian baker from having to bake a wedding cake—without considering the Christian wedding.

There are exceptional resources that explore the political rise of conservative Christianity and its hostile takeover of evangelicalism I encourage you to read. I am particularly fond of Kristin Kobes Du Mez's brilliant *Jesus and John Wayne: How White Evangelicals Corrupted a Faith and Fractured a Nation*, which explores evangelicalism's obsession with power and machismo; Jemar Tisby's *The Color of Compromise*, which details the American church's use of racist ideas for political power; and Talia Lavin's *Wild Faith: How the Christian Right Is Taking Over America*, which dives into the political and theological beliefs of a growing extremist movement.

The modern American evangelical project has deep roots in racism, from enslavement to the dismantling of Reconstruction to the creation of the Ku Klux Klan to the founding of private schools to avoid integration. This supremacist project is not only about race. Racism and ableism are directly linked through the eugenics movement, which was popular in the United States at the start of the twentieth century, and inspired Adolf Hitler's supremacist ambitions, including the Holocaust. Racists and eugenicists used the Bible and a perverted version of Christian theology to defend egregious violence and the inspiration for the mutilation of bodies, forced sterilizations, and genocide.

These acts and beliefs still continue, as some states link forced sterilization to welfare or to misdemeanor crimes, including a twenty-one-year-old woman who was sterilized in 2009 after a conviction for marijuana possession; and in 2018, an Oklahoma woman had a fraud conviction reduced after consenting to sterilization. Or consider the way the evangelical crusade against abortion is leading to the criminalization of miscarriage.

The Baptismal Covenant in *The Book of Common Prayer* asks each of us to "respect the dignity of every human being." In contrast, the malevolent acts of racist hatred, xenophobic fear, nationalistic violence, and psychological torture that supremacists and Christian nationalists offer are toward other children of God. These are children left to fend for themselves, historically underrepresented groups condemned for protecting each other. These are expectant mothers who have lost children. These are fathers working to provide for families and students going to school. This movement offers violence toward people we are called to love.

At the root of this brutality is not Christian belief itself but a vision of power that so poorly resembles the faith few should recognize it as faithful. In short, these people are seeking to "faithwash" cultural supremacy. This project is directly linked to what scholars refer to as the white power movement, an intentionally decentralized movement to encourage the separation of races and violent acts against the government for the creation of a white ethnostate. It is within this movement that we see aligned variations take flight, most infamously expressed in the bombing of the Alfred P. Murrah Federal Building (Oklahoma City) in 1994, the recurring murder of abortion providers, and in the rise of Christian nationalism in the United States and around the globe.

The hypocrisy involved in Christians killing for the sake of Jesus is so obvious to many that it can be hard to understand how people come to believe it. These convictions come, not from scripture or common belief, however, but from a sense of identity. An identity that is predominantly white and secure and permanently empowered. But just as we must hold onto our sense of community with our neighbors, we must remain faithful to the diversity within Christianity to see precisely where white supremacy and Christian nationalism itself, goes wrong.

Perhaps the place to start is with power itself.

KING JESUS

In the Gospels, Jesus has a complex relationship with power. Particularly with the holding and exercising of power, with the behavior and righteousness of the powerful, and with his own use of power. Jesus uses the language of kingdoms, often contrasting the Kingdom of God or the Kingdom of Heaven with the kingdoms of earth. He speaks of commands, reign, and the power of God to be above us and beyond human reach. And yet, his harshest critiques are to the powerful, often in the same breath as forgiving the deeply sinful. This might cause no small amount of confusion, perhaps. Though I wouldn't suggest it ought to.

DREW DOWNS

The Gospels are deeply anti-supremacy. Jesus avoids all attempts by crowds to crown him king, and by Satan who, during the temptation in the wilderness, attempts to convince Jesus to claim power over others, the environment, and God. This anti-supremacy nature of the Gospels makes the Christian nationalist and white supremacy project a kind of paradox. They seek to control everything in the name of Jesus that Jesus specifically rejects. There are five areas of our lives in which Christian nationalists seek supremacy: politics, ethnicity, economics, theology, and culture.

Christian nationalism seeks to unify church and state under a single, centralized authority, claiming a divine right of kings. This is why the far-right political theorist Curtis Yarvin is stirring up desire for a monarchy; it would unify control under a king and strip authority from our democratic systems. Yarvin's rise among the politically powerful demonstrates the willingness within the movement to entertain ideas otherwise forbidden from public discussion—precisely because they represent a fundamental rejection of the democratic project.

In Matthew 25, Jesus teaches his followers that it is their action, not the king's, that matters to God. In describing a time of judgment, he says that when they feed the hungry, give drink to the thirsty, welcome the stranger, clothe the naked, care for the sick, and visit the imprisoned, they are doing this to Jesus. And when they refuse these to anyone, they refuse them to Jesus.

Jesus does not offer a vision of political supremacy, but of caring for the weakest. Much like his own rejection of supreme power, we must reject supreme power. And further, as we see others suffering, we are to recognize it as suffering and work to transform systems of injustice.

ETHNIC CONTROL

Christian nationalists follow the white power movement's focus on controlling the ethnic makeup of the country. Modern evangelicalism inherited a history of racism that can be traced to a time pre-dating the founding of the country; the evidence can be found in segregation academies and plantations throughout the southern United States.

In *Stand Your Ground: Black Bodies and the Justice of God*, the Rev. Dr. Kelly Brown Douglas traces the modern conservative evangelical movement's relationship with race through its adoration of Anglo-Saxon culture, seeing themselves as the inheritors of the Greek philosophical tradition. Twentieth century eugenicists, describing the superiority of white people, drew a straight line through themselves all the way back to Plato, arguing that anything good in the world came from this line, these people, from Greece, to Rome, to the Anglo-Saxons, to the English, to America. Today's eugenicist-inspired nationalists are aping this same superiority pose, focusing on what they call classical education and decrying attempts to read those who stand outside the white western canon while speaking about declining birth rates and erasing diversity initiatives.

In the Gospel of Luke, when a lawyer asks Jesus what he must do to inherit eternal life—love your neighbor as yourself. So, the man asks Jesus, "Who is my neighbor?" His answer is a parable we refer to as "The Good Samaritan," a teaching that still scandalizes the delicate dispositions of the powerful as much now as it did then.

In the story, it isn't a righteous man who helps the wounded, abused, and beaten traveler, mugged and left for dead on the road to Jerusalem, it is a foreigner. And not just any foreigner—a Samaritan, from the tribe

Judeans labeled as the enemy. And for good reason: they had a century of bitter, intractable fights between these two regional neighbors. Casting the hero of his parable as coming from outside his disciples' ethnic group, Jesus hoped to shatter the monoethnic control of the dominant culture and encourage us to see the common humanity of our neighbors.

ECONOMIC CONTROL

While matters of race and politics are front and center in the public imagination, Christian nationalist ideology also seeks to exert economic control over the nation and its inhabitants. This is, in part, due to its associations with libertarian and neoliberal economic principles, which concern themselves ostensibly with personal responsibility and local control. But these factors represent a means of controlling the fortunes of other people and how we talk about it, seeking to make Christian synonymous with conservative.

Today's conservative evangelicals argue that Christianity is not only compatible with modern capitalism, but glorified by it, suggesting that capitalism itself is God-inspired, rather than a human means of ordering society. This attachment to capitalism blinds many people of faith from seeing just how different Jesus's economic priorities are.

The parable Jesus tells in Matthew 20:1-16 reveals an entirely different economic theory. A landowner seeks laborers to work in his vineyard. He keeps hiring throughout the day, then, when the day is done, he pays everyone a day's wage. He doesn't pay people more for working longer—he pays them all a day's wage. The first laborers expect to be paid more, for they did more work. But the parable intends to draw us away from merit, circumstance, and comparison, the hallmarks of an economic system designed to divide and produce poverty and instead redirects us toward a vision of equity and protection—one that ensures, as we pray in his prayer, that everyone receive their daily bread.   DREW DOWNS

THEOLOGICAL CONTROL

As a part of the modern evangelical movement, Christian nationalism seeks to replace the diversity in the Christian theological tradition with their view of scripture, tradition, and mission. This is evident in many areas, but most clearly in matters of sex and gender, which have been an obsession of the religious right since the 1980s when the evangelical movement initiated an opposition to abortion and the rights of LGBTQIA+ people. But just as important in our analysis is public complicity in allowing this movement to code anti-abortion and anti-gay convictions as de facto Christian, rather than the priority of a particular subset. It has never been true to say that all Christians are against abortion or gay rights or that opposition to them is the central message of our faith.

As if to counter the exclusivist and supremacist ideologies, Jesus offers a collection of three parables in

Luke 15, which describe the urgency of searching for the lost and celebrating in finding them. In the first, Jesus speaks of the shepherd who leaves a whole flock of sheep to search for one that is lost. In the second, he describes a woman who loses a coin (worth a day's wages) and lights lamps to search for it through the night. In the final, Jesus describes two brothers, one who runs away and is forgiven by his father and another who, out of fury at his father's generosity and selfish jealousy for not being spoiled in comparison, threatens to storm off in the end.

Given the unforgiving, abusive, supremacist ideology of Christian nationalism, it is almost as if they haven't read Jesus's most compelling words about mercy and joy, reuniting families torn apart by abusive assumptions, and celebrating with joy when we are who we are together.

CULTURAL CONTROL

Christian nationalism's clearest attempt to control is in the culture, through legislatures, executives, and the courts; through language, education, and media; and even in reshaping our understanding of right and wrong. We've seen this movement justify torture and war when their Lord preaches nonviolence and peace. We've seen them justify the abuse, kidnapping, and imprisonment of foreigners when their Lord preaches welcome to them. Hatred, exclusion, exploitation: all concepts vilified by Jesus are being championed as a justified means. A means to control.

The Gospels are full of examples that reject such acts as evil. One story sticks out for me, however. In the fourth chapter of John, Jesus is on his way home, and instead of doing what most Judeans did then, which was to go around Samaria, he chose to go through it. He sits beside a well there and has a scandalous conversation with a woman, getting to know her, sharing with her. When Jesus's disciples want him to leave, he says, nah, let's stay a few days. It is not a story of conversion and dominance, of vilification and hatred, or any grotesque attempt to conquer one's way to control, but a story of community and conversation, of intimacy and connection. And Jesus does this by countering the cultural priorities of dominance and control by crossing political, ethnic, economic, theological, and cultural boundaries to find a shared common space with others in light of their differences.

There are so many examples in the Gospels of Jesus rejecting dominance, control, and supremacy. One of the sayings we can find in each of the Gospels, the first shall be last and the last shall be first, demonstrates Jesus's desire for his followers to reorder our own relationship to dominance in our world. He teaches about protecting children and listening to children, being like children—not dominating and controlling them. In the Beatitudes, Jesus argues that blessing doesn't come from wealth or power or reward us with gilded extravagance, but comes from empathy and compassion, meekness and mourning, hungering and thirsting for righteousness, mercy and peacemaking.

Supremacy is sin and deeply anti-Christ. Christians who follow Jesus's way of love recognize that hate is not love, supremacy is not humility, war is not peace, genocide is not healing, and dominance is not hope. Christian nationalism is culture war propaganda used to destroy political, ethnic, economic, theological, and cultural diversity and claim total control of the world.

What then do we do?

Thankfully the simplest response is also the most effective: Don't buy it. Embrace our diversity as common and encourage our neighbors to join us. See the humanity of everyone and recognize that each is our neighbor. And as Jesus says, "let your yes be yes and your no be no," for we can see what is love and what is not. And we can live like it.

As a Christian, I pray the Lord's Prayer each day—praying that the grace of heaven would be the way of the world; that I and everyone else, has enough food today and tomorrow, because it is our right; that all my debts be forgiven because I (hopefully) have already forgiven the debts others owe me; and for protection from evil because this is God's kingdom, not ours. In short, I pray for things Christian nationalists reject. I pray for solidarity and equity through the sharing of Jesus's love. And that looks a lot more like what Jesus teaches.

Drew Downs is an Episcopal priest and an MFA student in creative writing at Alma College in Alma, Michigan. He writes creative nonfiction and poetry and was the recipient of the Irish Benevolent Society preaching award from Huron University College. He currently serves a congregation in Indiana committed to ending homelessness, food insecurity, racism, and the death penalty.

PART V

Resilience in Resistance

Chapter 13

Strategies for Coping with the Impact of What Is Happening in Our World

By Joan Adams, msw, lcsw-r

I F YOU STARTED this book from the beginning, what you've read so far is a charting of the chaos and the undermining of democracy in this country. You've read about formation of the earliest democracies and the factors that precipitate their end, not to mention the ways different movements have undermined the promise of America. You've also read about specific legislation and concerted efforts by citizens that have propelled us forward in our struggle to become a more perfect union. And, you read how all of this has directly impacted people from a legal and social point of view. Now let's take a look at various ways the current state of our country may impact *you* (your emotions, your thoughts, and your body) and ways you can handle the impacts you experience.

I am a Black American woman therapist and a consultant to organizations about racial/ethnic/gender identity and the impact of racism and other forms of oppression. The perspectives and strategies I will offer you may seem obvious, and that's good because these are all steps that anyone can take. They may also provide you with new perspectives and approaches, or leave you feeling challenged. They're things I use in my work and with myself. I ask that you open your heart and your mind, and bring your curiosity and apply what may be useful to you in this arduous time.

STRATEGIES
FOR COPING WITH
THE IMPACT
OF WHAT
IS HAPPENING
IN OUR WORLD

REFLECTING ON WHAT IS HAPPENING

Start by noticing and acknowledging that what is going on around you is real. For many of us, what we value and who we hold dear are indeed under attack. There is an attempt to dismantle institutions and eject people we care about from the country. People are losing their jobs, their homes, their loved ones, and some are losing their lives.

A scene comes to mind that serves as an analogy for what we're all experiencing. Imagine standing on a beach, seeing huge waves crashing ashore and creating an undertow that's dragging people out to sea. You don't know how to rescue the people being caught in the undertow and you are frightened the next wave may take you out to sea. The next thing you know, you're surrounded by water, far from the shore flailing, disoriented.

When we human beings are faced with a reality that is frightening or overwhelming, we experience fear and stress in our bodies, our minds, and our emotions. Our experience of a present frightening situation is also influenced by past experiences where we have been frightened or hurt.

JOAN ADAMS, MSW, LCSW-R

If our body and mind experience the stressful situation as traumatic, we may have a trauma response. The response to trauma is typically either: fight, flee, freeze, or fawn. There is no right or wrong way to respond, but the response is often immediate, without us planning or being fully aware of our response. But the good news is there are ways to reorient ourselves and to make it back to dry land. When we are aware of the "wave" and our reaction to the danger, what we can do is stop, notice our reactions, and remind ourselves to breathe. This helps our bodies to interrupt our automatic responses to stress or trauma.

In addition to our internal individual responses to frightening or stressful experiences, we each exist in the context of our family and friends, our work, school, and neighborhood community, and the larger society. We are each impacted by these various contexts and by the history of these systems. We might think of ourselves and the contextual systems in which we exist as concentric circles. Each level of the circles can provide us with support or leave us struggling on our own. For example, if you suddenly lose your job due to governmental budget cuts, you may rely on your family and friends for financial help and encouragement. At the same time, governmental unemployment benefits and health insurance (Medicaid) may be limited or unavailable.

STRATEGIES
FOR COPING WITH
THE IMPACT
OF WHAT
IS HAPPENING
IN OUR WORLD

Many of us notice that when the world around us becomes chaotic or frightening and threatens our access to basic needs of adequate food, shelter, and connections with others, we think and feel we are the problem. We may feel we are not doing enough; we are "crazy" to feel so overwhelmed; or we want to stop trying to perform at work or school. We may experience symptoms of depression: feeling sad, low energy, having difficulty getting enough sleep, eating more or less than we need, feeling easily irritated, and withdrawing from our usual contacts with friends and family. While any of these symptoms and feelings may be a result of your personal circumstances, such as a recent loss of family member, friend, or position at work or school, these feelings may also be a response to the chaos in the world around you that is described in this book.

First of all, you are not crazy, and the problem is not you. You, like the rest of us, are in the midst of the very powerful, chaotic set of circumstances as presented in this book. We are being overloaded at lightning speed with actions that are dismantling services, social structures, and institutions. You are under attack. Your body is under attack. Your emotions are under attack. The fact that many of us are feeling some version of "What's wrong with me?" or "Why can't I manage things better" or "I am not enough" should come as no surprise. Whatever your circumstances or your behavior, know that you are not causing what is going on. You can then reframe the question from, "What's wrong with me?" to "What is happening to all of us and how is that affecting me and those around me?"

UNDERSTANDING RACISM AND ITS IMPACT

JOAN ADAMS,
MSW, LCSW-R

A major aspect of stress and trauma is the impact of systemic racism on Black, Brown, and Asian people. While much has changed since the legal segregation of Black and white people, or the racial violence of lynching and the burning down of whole Black towns (Tulsa, Oklahoma, for example), the internment of Japanese Americans during World War II, or the sterilization of Puerto Rican women without their knowledge, racism is still very much alive and its impact on People of Color continues to be felt today.

We are all witness to and impacted by the current demonization and violent removal of Latine immigrants. Families and individuals who are and have been contributing to the economy and well-being of everyone living in the United States are being terrified by raids carried out by armed, unidentified men at places of business such as restaurants, farms, factories, and even churches and schools.

Another important aspect of the stress and traumatic impact of racism is the intergenerational effects of racism.

The grandchildren and great-grandchildren of folks who experienced the various manifestations of racial violence mentioned above carry the emotional weight of their ancestors, seen and treated as less than fully human and subjected to racial violence.

This intergenerational impact of racial stress and trauma exists alongside current manifestations of racism. These include inequitable access to quality healthcare in poor Black or Brown communities, higher high school drop-out rates for Black boys, greater difficulty for working and middle-class Black people securing mortgage loans to buy homes, and the forcible ejection of Latine people regardless of their American citizenship or length of time contributing to this country.

One resource I recommend to readers about how to heal racialized trauma is *My Grandmother's Hands: Racialized Trauma and the Pathway to Mending Our Hearts and Bodies*, by Resmaa Menakem.

GROUNDING, CENTERING EXERCISE

Now let's look at some things you can do to manage the impact of what is happening to your body, mind, and spirit.

When you find yourself feeling overwhelmed, here is an exercise you can do to shut out the noise, calm down, focus on what you can do, and reset yourself in the moment. Another way of describing the purpose of this exercise is to get yourself centered and present in the moment. You can use this exercise alone or in a group that is meeting to work together. If it is a group, invite the whole group to use this practice at the beginning of your time together.

STEP ONE: Find a place where you can be quiet and uninterrupted for about five minutes. I know that is a challenge for many of us. Here are some possible places you can find a quiet space to be alone: during a coffee break, take the coffee outside or to a quiet spot at your workplace; a bathroom (at home, not at your job or school where the bathroom is public); while walking outside for five to ten minutes; or sitting in your car alone. You might use part of a meal break to be in any of these spaces. Use your own creativity to discover a quiet space that will work in your environment and circumstances.

JOAN ADAMS, MSW, LCSW-R

STEP TWO: Sit comfortably in a chair or on a seat with your back against the chair and your feet solidly planted on the floor or ground, and drop your shoulders down so they are relaxed and not tense. Remind yourself that you are being solidly and well supported by Mother Earth who supports us all.

STEP THREE: Pay attention to your body. Mentally scan your body to see how every part of your body is feeling at this moment. Notice where you are feeling tension and where you may be feeling relaxed or energized. Start at the tips of your toes; work your way up to your ankles; your shins; your thighs; your groin; your hips; your butt; your midsection; your chest; your shoulders; your arms, wrists, and hands; the cords of your neck (where many of us carry tension); your jaw; your temples and the bones under and above your eyes (where many of us experience sinus discomfort or pain); and up to the top of your head. You are noticing, without judgment, how your body is feeling.

Again, notice where in your body you feel any tightness, tension, discomfort, or even pain. Also notice where you may be feeling some relaxation or positive energy.

STEP FOUR: Be aware of the space where you are sitting and the energy of that space.

STRATEGIES
FOR COPING WITH
THE IMPACT
OF WHAT
IS HAPPENING
IN OUR WORLD

STEP FIVE: Be aware of and open to the energy of the Universe, the life force. If you have a spiritual belief and/or practice, be open to the life force of the Divine. You might think of the life force energy coming in through the top of your head.

STEP SIX: Then, making no judgments about any of this, open your eyes and take in who may be in the space around you. (If you are doing this Centering Exercise in a group that is working together, make eye contact with each person in the group.)

STEP SEVEN: Take three deep breaths and exhale fully. Notice when you feel fully present to yourself and your surroundings.

STEP EIGHT: To yourself or to the group, say that you are fully present and ready to start whatever you are about to do (e.g., start a work or school assignment, clean a room, participate in a meeting, start your day, make a call or have a meeting about something you are feeling anxious about, get your children up and ready for the day).

As you start the individual or group task from a more centered, present place, you will notice that you have more energy and less anxiety as you engage in the task before you. You might check in with yourself silently as you engage in the task or group to notice the level of your energy and attention. If you find yourself feeling bodily or emotional tension, or telling yourself something negative, take a minute to relax your shoulders, take three deep breaths, and fully exhale. This will relax your diaphragm and help you get more centered as you pursue your task.

JOAN ADAMS,
MSW, LCSW-R

ACKNOWLEDGE AND TALK ABOUT WHAT'S GOING ON

Beyond being centered and present to your experience and your surroundings, one thing that is helpful in coping with chaos, stress, and even traumatic events, is finding a group of people you feel comfortable and compatible with to talk to about what is happening. The group could be as simple as friends who already get together for an activity or to hang out. You can take a few minutes in your group to check in and share how everybody is doing in the current stress and chaos. It is also important to familiarize oneself and share with others in your group the historical and current manifestations of racial disparities, inequities, and violence.

Having a safe group with whom you can share your reactions to the current stressful conditions is enormously helpful because then you're not sitting alone, in your head, in your body, with all this "stuff" that's having a traumatizing impact on people. If you don't have a group, here are some suggestions about how to find one.

FINDING AND CONNECTING WITH COMMUNITY

STRATEGIES
FOR COPING WITH
THE IMPACT
OF WHAT
IS HAPPENING
IN OUR WORLD

Take a moment to note what informal or formal groups you already belong to. It may be other parents with whom you share childcare resources or who have children in the same schools. It may be a neighborhood group that meets to discuss issues like traffic concerns or activities like the upkeep of green spaces. You may be part of a group at your place of worship, or your professional association or union. It may be a group of friends who meet in person, online or via Zoom to hang out and share space with each other. Other groups you may already belong to include a therapy group or a twelve-step group such as Alcoholics Anonymous, Al-Anon, or Adult Children of Alcoholics.

Regularly attending any of those groups will help you stay more centered, share your experiences with others, hear that you are not alone, and share with others how everyone is coping with the stress of the current chaos. You can also encourage group members to come to meetings, if you notice they stopped attending. Reaching out to help others also activates endorphins, which are hormones that give us a feeling of calm, satisfaction, and pleasure.

If you do not have a group you can meet with regularly, you could initiate one by inviting a few friends, colleagues, or family members to check in with each other regularly. The group might connect by regularly engaging in an activity that everyone is interested in, like walking, visiting outdoor spaces, attending cultural or sporting events, or having a meal together.

If there's not a group you can join in person, create an online group of people you know and are already comfortable with, that you can contact so you don't have to face all of this by yourself.

I know families whose members are spread around the country or around the world. They set up a family WhatsApp group, and they meet regularly, often at least once a week. It's a great way use of technology to stay in touch with one another.

JOAN ADAMS, MSW, LCSW-R

Male readers may have been socialized to feel, "Nah, I'm good. I'm a man. I don't do therapy. I don't have time for all that sissy stuff." Thing is, most men already have groups they regularly engage with—for sports, card games, fishing, etc. You may not think of those spaces as group activities, yet in those groups men often have conversations about what's going on in the world around them. You might remind yourself, "I have a community, a group I already belong to, and they help my mind, my body, and my soul deal with all this craziness." The point is that there are already things men do that they don't necessarily think of as therapeutic, but they are absolutely feeling the positive benefit.

Sometimes it's a challenge to decide whether to bring socio-political topics into any of the groups I've mentioned above. Whether you do or do not is dependent on the make-up of the particular group and your relationship with the group members. You don't want to risk blowing up your spot in the group by bringing up the realities that everyone is seeking respite from. On the other hand, you're reminding yourself that the group is restorative to you. Within that particular group, you get some "time out" and get refilled. Maybe you address it to the group in a way that says, "Hey, we're going to check in with one another and how we're dealing with all the craziness going on now."

What I'm saying is that if you have a group that focuses on a particular activity or common interest, realize you're already a part of a community that helps you survive or stay emotionally regulated—and by that I mean it keeps you from becoming so depressed or enraged that you act out. The group also offers an opportunity to rally around others in the group who are directly impacted by the current chaos.

Whether your group is a community gardening group, parents of toddlers, or guys who regularly play basketball, when folks get together they are going to say to each other in their own way, "How's it going?" Having that space to both check on others and be supported by others is a major way to help manage the challenges around us.

In these times, if you don't have a group space like that, you might start looking for one. Or you can find a person you could start checking in with. If you're more isolated, and are more online, is there anyone you chat with who feels safe, or with whom you have a common interest who could be a person you check in with?

Opportunities to build connections also exist in volunteering, community service, and mentoring. When you take time out to give, you're also receiving. Use your gifts, skills, and information to give back. By giving back, you're validating your own lived experience. There are a lot of things in someone's lived experience that have helped them become successful in their personal, work, and student life. A lot of people feel they don't have anything to offer, but when they look at their life, their experiences, and accomplishments, they begin to realize all they have to offer.

JOAN ADAMS,
MSW, LCSW-R

RESISTING THE CHAOS AROUND YOU

When we are faced with circumstances that are hurtful, demeaning, and overwhelming, we can easily feel that we are stuck with the circumstances and have no power to resist. Resistance to the current chaos is life-affirming, can restore our sense of agency, and can help to change the harmful, overwhelming circumstances. A form of resistance that we all see on television and social media in this current environment is public demonstrations that protest the treatment of Latine folks being physically taken from our communities by unidentified armed men and then sent to jails and detention centers that are often far away. No notice or information is being given to their families about where the loved one has been sent. Neither the person nor their family has an opportunity to challenge in court the person's seizure and transportation to detention centers.

In addition to protest demonstrations, we often think of resistance as political activism, ranging from writing or calling elected politicians to protesting government practice or laws, or various forms of civil disobedience (like the Civil Rights sit-ins to protest segregated lunch counters). I refer you to an often-missed but very important form of resistance, which is *rest*. Tricia Hersey has described the importance of us getting enough rest as a part of any resistance we engage in. Her two books are: *Rest Is Resistance: A Manifesto* and *Rest Is Resistance: Free Yourself from Grind Culture and Reclaim Your Life*.

STRATEGIES
FOR COPING WITH
THE IMPACT
OF WHAT
IS HAPPENING
IN OUR WORLD

There are two other effective ways that you can regain your balance and centeredness in the midst of the current chaos:

1. Engage with creativity, yours and others, and
2. Build and maintain intergenerational connections.

EXPRESS YOURSELF

Creativity in any form—painting, sculpture, writing, music, dance, poetry—is powerfully restorative. One thing that people who use their gifts to produce creative works can do is to maintain their integrity about what they're seeing and feeling in the world around them, and reflect what they and many of us aspire to. Artists have an enormous power in doing that. If you are not an artist, you can actively look for and read books and/or magazines and go to exhibits and performances. Consciously take in the creative output of artists to replenish, refresh, and keep yourself sane. Artists are an enormous resource to the rest of us.

Actively engage in the output of artists of every stripe. Music, for example, can be enormously healing. So in the midst of all this chaos, whatever music soothes and enlivens and feeds you—listen to it. This is another way to cope with all this craziness and not withdraw from the world. Or find some other things that are important to you. No matter where you live, even if you don't have direct access to exhibits, you can access all sorts of creative work online.

JOAN ADAMS, MSW, LCSW-R

INTERGENERATIONAL CONNECTIONS

Don't get stuck in your own age group. Actively seek out and use your intergenerational connections. The benefits aren't just that young people gain wisdom and older people become revitalized. Intergenerational connections work in both directions. Older people gain wisdom and insights from younger people's fresh perspectives and younger people can be revitalized and even pulled back from the brink of depression by learning about and sharing all the activities seniors are involved in.

"This is what you're doing, senior person? This is your story? I'm twenty-five sitting around feeling depressed. You're seventy-five and you're around here doing what?? You're doing all this?!"

A SUMMARY OF THE COPING STRATEGIES
PRESENTED IN THIS CHAPTER

STRATEGIES

FOR COPING WITH

THE IMPACT

OF WHAT

IS HAPPENING

IN OUR WORLD

1. Get yourself grounded—either alone, with a good friend, or in a group.
2. Recognize the reality of what's happening and that you are not causing this. It's not that you're not doing enough or you aren't capable enough, smart enough, or creative enough. You're not feeling overwhelmed because of your inadequacy.

   You are feeling overwhelmed because what's happening to you is everything you've read about in this book so far. You are feeling overwhelmed, sad, defeated or angry because you, I, and everyone you care about—and even a few people you may not care about—are experiencing a tidal wave of physical, psychological, and emotional chaos.
3. Connect with other people you feel safe with and talk about what you are seeing and experiencing. Naming what is frightening or stressing you is enormously therapeutic. Also share with those same people how you and they may be feeling inadequate, overwhelmed, and even responsible for what is going on. Then share how each of you is coping with the current chaos.
4. Recognize and share with your trusted others the ways that chaos has appeared for you, your people, and other people over several generations. Especially recognize and share the ways that earlier generations have resisted and maintained their balance in the face of earlier hurt and violence. That may have happened

in this country or in places where your ancestors lived before arriving here.

Acknowledge that some folks and their ancestors have been hurt and traumatized for so long that, in layman's terms, they're not thinking straight. They may just accept the reality of being harmed as inevitable: "It's just the way it is for us." They may not be aware of the resources available to them, let alone be using them. So in that regard, the tidal wave is working the way it is supposed to.

JOAN ADAMS,
MSW, LCSW-R

5. It is important to remember that cycles of oppression and harm exist along with cycles of resistance, and that there are lessons to be learned from ancestors, our own and others, about how to resist. We do not need to feel we can do nothing.

6. Resistance is life affirming and can change things. We can each find our place and ways of resisting. Resistance is an important part of healing. Resistance is a way to take care of yourself and loved ones, and a way to recover from harm.

You can engage in resistance in many ways. You can go out and organize and demonstrate with others; you can help others by volunteering with groups that offer care, like providing food, running errands for folks who have limited capacity to do that for themselves, tutoring, or mentoring. If you are already doing some of these caring things, remind yourself that these are all expressions of being in a community and of resistance. And remember that giving yourself enough rest is a form of resistance.

This chapter is all about maintaining your center, your balance, and your certainty about your own humanity in the midst of all of these moves that can destroy human connections. These are strategies anyone can use. When we are in the midst of feeling stressed or traumatized, even if we've learned these strategies before, the information can go out the window. So when you notice you are feeling overwhelmed, or hopeless, remind yourself of what you know and what you've learned here.

STRATEGIES
FOR COPING WITH
THE IMPACT
OF WHAT
IS HAPPENING
IN OUR WORLD

Some people have never learned this perspective or these strategies. All they have received are the most negative messages about who they are as a Black person, as a Latine woman, as a Person of Color, as someone from a low-income family, as a person living with a disability, as someone who has made life decisions that got them into trouble, or as someone who has lived in less than ideal circumstances. Some of these negative messages have come from parents, grandparents, or people they hung out with, because those folks have been overwhelmed and received negative messages. Sometimes the negative messages have led to folks not realizing or forgetting the coping strategies that they and their ancestors have in fact used.

These exercises and strategies are reminders of the human capacity to remain resilient even in the most adverse circumstances. Just know you're not the problem, and practice ways to cope.

Joan Adams, MSW, LCSW-R is a licensed clinical social worker in Harlem, New York, providing psychotherapy, clinical supervision, training, and consultation on race and racism for organizations and individuals. She co-facilitates an international group for BIPOC therapists who are exploring the use of Systems Centered Therapy in their work. Ms. Adams is also a Warden on the Vestry of the Episcopal Congregation of St. Saviour, the resident congregation at the Cathedral of St. John the Divine.

Chapter 14

No Slingshot Required

By SHARON PENDANA

THROUGHOUT THE AGES, humanity has taken a stand against injustice. When faced with intolerable situations and untenable systems, we resist. This uniquely human pursuit of justice, deeply rooted in our nature as social beings, has given rise to generations of resistance movements. Each is a collective donning of liberatory capes to right the wrongs of our time. The successful ones—characterized by strategic, disciplined execution—persist through mass participation, shaping history by challenging injustice through unified action.

Resistance, whether through force or peaceful means, demands profound courage, steadfast conviction, and unshakable resolve. Nonviolent resistance, in particular, requires an inner stillness—maintaining calm in the face of violence and equilibrium in its aftermath. As Thoreau asserts in his influential 1849 essay "Civil Disobedience," we must "not lend" ourselves "to the wrong which" we "condemn." Likewise, Gandhi's commitment to Ahimsa—the principle of non-harm, grounded in Hindu, Buddhist, and Jain traditions— rejects violence as a means of change, urging moral strength over aggression.

The following sections, each introduced by a movement rallying cry, examine impactful movements that used peaceful direct action. Driven by the collective strength of individuals united for a cause, these movements used boycotts, selective patronage, civil disobedience, noncooperation, petitioning, and demonstrations—picketing, sit-ins, vigils, strikes, and fasting—to uphold human dignity while sparking change.

NO BREAD, NO WORK

The global quest for justice predates modern times. As early as the twelfth century BCE, Egyptian tomb builders at Deir el-Medina collectively ceased work until they received overdue compensation, primarily in the form of grain rations, history's first recorded labor strike. Their successful sit-in protest reveals the deep roots of peaceful resistance.

Youth have long stood at the forefront of peaceful resistance, embodying the intersectionality and dynamism of social movements throughout the past century. Their energy, passion, and indomitable will have infused justice struggles with new vitality, igniting and sustaining transformative change.

GREENSBORO FOUR AND THE RISE OF SNCC. In 1960, four Black college students "sat-in" at a segregated Woolworth's counter in Greensboro, North Carolina. Denied service, they stayed until closing—defying the waiter, manager, and a police officer—and returned the next day with supporters. Within days, hundreds joined.

Recognizing the power of student-led resistance, activist Ella Baker organized a youth summit that gave rise to the Student Nonviolent Coordinating Committee (SNCC), led by activists such as Diane Nash and John Lewis. SNCC pioneered sit-ins, Freedom Rides, Jail-no-bail strategies, and voter drives, confronting white supremacy through organized, peaceful disruption.

SCHOOL STRIKE FOR CLIMATE. On August 20, 2018, fifteen-year-old Greta Thunberg, frustrated by inattention to the climate crisis, sat outside Stockholm's Parliament House, demanding urgent action to limit global warming. She returned daily for the three weeks leading to the Swedish election. Soon, other students joined. With the hashtag #FridaysforFuture, the campaign went viral,

SHARON
PENDANA

uniting millions in over 200 countries in climate activism. Her tenacity shows how individual action can drive global change.

NO SLINGSHOT
REQUIRED

"The time has come for action" served as the rallying cry of the American Abolition Movement. While some resistance efforts took violent forms—such as Nat Turner's revolt or John Brown's raid—most relied on peaceful tactics, including petitions, rallies, antislavery publications, and boycotts of goods made by enslaved labor.

Religious communities played a unifying role in the abolitionist movement. The African Methodist Episcopal Church and Quakers, among others, framed abolition as a moral imperative, mobilizing those who might not have otherwise engaged and broadening the movement's reach and impact.

GARRISON, DOUGLASS, & TUBMAN. American abolitionism reached its height in the 1830s when William Lloyd Garrison launched *The Liberator*, a newspaper dedicated to ending slavery. Two years later, he co-founded the American Anti-Slavery Society. Frederick Douglass escaped enslavement in 1838 and rose to prominence through powerful oratory and writing, shifting public opinion by adding a deeply personal perspective to the national conversation. In 1847, he founded *The North Star* to further the abolitionist cause.

Undeterred by oppressive laws, abolitionists continued to petition and protest. The Fugitive Slave Act of
1850, mandating the return of escaped enslaved people,
provoked widespread outrage and intensified activism.
Harriet Tubman, a formidable conductor on the Underground Railroad—a clandestine network of escape
routes and safe houses—led seventy enslaved people to
freedom on thirteen missions. During the Civil War, she
bravely helped lead a Union raid that liberated over 700
more in June 1863.

Although Lincoln's Emancipation Proclamation declared freedom for enslaved people in Confederate states,
enslavement remained legal elsewhere until the Thirteenth Amendment passed in 1865, abolishing enslavement throughout the United States.

SHARON
PENDANA

LABOR RIGHTS

Rapid industrialization created harsh labor conditions
as the U.S. population tripled between 1860 and 1910.
Organized labor became the antidote to exploitative
workplaces. The American Federation of Labor (AFL),
formed in 1886, fought to secure workers' rights and
fair wages.

By the 1930s, the labor movement was in full swing.
In 1935, the United Auto Workers formed to advocate
for auto laborers. During the 1936–1937 Flint sit-down
strike, General Motors workers refused to leave the fac-
tory, blocking strikebreakers. This pivotal action led to
widespread unionization and the enactment of labor

laws, such as the Fair Labor Standards Act (1938), which established minimum wage, overtime pay, and child labor protections.

HUELGA MEANS STRIKE! In September 1965, Filipino and Mexican farmworkers in California's grape-growing San Joaquin Valley united in a shared struggle for better wages and working conditions. Ironically, when Mexican workers had previously organized strikes, growers typically recruited Filipino grape pickers as strikebreakers.

Despite this history, Larry Itliong led fellow Filipino farmworkers in protesting pay cuts and harsh conditions—including pesticide exposure and inadequate shelter—and appealed to Mexican-American migrant labor advocates César Chávez and Dolores Huerta to join forces. In August 1966, the coalition formed United Farm Workers.

Inspired by the Montgomery Bus Boycott, in 1965 the Delano Grape Strike employed peaceful picketing and a consumer boycott of grapes to pressure growers. Despite violence and intimidation, strikers upheld an ethos of nonviolence. After five years of sustained protest, grape growers met the farmworkers' demands—a watershed moment in both agricultural and labor history.

FREEDOM NOW! AMERICAN CIVIL RIGHTS MOVEMENT

Despite Reconstruction-era amendments that abolished enslavement, established citizenship, and granted voting rights to all male citizens, a regressive backlash—

including violent reprisals and the rise of Jim Crow laws—undermined these gains and curtailed Black freedoms.

The 1908 Springfield Race Riot in Illinois, marked by white mob violence, prompted an interracial coalition to form the National Association for the Advancement of Colored People in 1909. Change came slowly, but it grew to become the largest civil rights organization in the U.S. In 1942, students at the University of Chicago founded the Congress of Racial Equality (CORE), planting seeds of modern civil resistance.

SHARON
PENDANA

The Honorable John R. Lewis dedicated his life to advancing civil and human rights, from grassroots student activism to a long tenure in the U.S. House of Representatives. He championed key laws like the Voting Rights Advancement Act, the Emmett Till Antilynching Act, and the Equality Act. Lewis also fought for criminal justice reform, health equity, immigration rights, gun safety, marriage equality, education, and racial and economic justice. Known for his courage, compassion, and unwavering commitment to nonviolence, this civil rights icon and elder statesman of the movement is remembered for his enduring call to "get into good trouble, necessary trouble" in pursuit of justice and equality.

MONTGOMERY BUS BOYCOTT. Rosa Parks' arrest for boldly refusing to give up her seat on a segregated bus catalyzed a year-long bus boycott. In the highly organized campaign led by Rev. Dr. Martin Luther King Jr., about eighty percent of Montgomery's Black residents walked, carpooled, and refused to ride public buses from December 1, 1955, to December 20, 1956. The grassroots movement inflicted substantial economic losses on the bus system and ultimately led to a victory: a Supreme Court ruling that declared segregation on public transit unconstitutional.

FREEDOM RIDES. After the success with municipal buses, CORE then targeted the interstate bus industry's defiance of a 1946 Supreme Court ruling banning segregation in interstate travel. They organized interracial groups to ride buses through the South, testing the law. The first Freedom Ride departed Washington, D.C., in May 1961 with thirteen riders, including twenty-one-year-old John Lewis. Riders faced arrests and savage violence, including a firebombing in Anniston, Alabama. Prioritizing safety, CORE ended the ride early and flew riders to New Orleans for a planned rally.

Unwilling to let the momentum die, SNCC's Diane Nash mobilized a second wave of riders, continuing the mission. Singing songs of freedom, they endured beatings as authorities failed to intervene. Their courage and determination pressured the federal government to enforce desegregation in interstate travel later that year. Over six months, 436 Freedom Riders participated in more than sixty trips—laying the groundwork for future civil rights activism.

THE MARCH ON WASHINGTON. On June 12, 1963, just hours after President Kennedy's civil rights address,

NAACP Field Secretary Medgar Evers was assassinated in Mississippi, the tragedy highlighting the urgent need for sweeping reforms. Eleven weeks later, over 250,000 people gathered for the March on Washington for Jobs and Freedom, the largest assembly in the city's history. Organized by A. Philip Randolph and Bayard Rustin, the event was the first televised march, solidifying Rev. Dr. Martin Luther King Jr.'s leadership of the civil rights movement with his famed "I Have a Dream" speech. This historic moment drew global attention to the civil rights struggle in the U.S.

SHARON
PENDANA

The American Civil Rights Movement achieved great strides in moving the needle toward equality: landmark legislation included the Civil Rights Act of 1964, outlawing discrimination based on race, color, religion, sex, or national origin, and the Voting Rights Act of 1965, prohibiting discriminatory voting practices. John Lewis would become a civil rights icon, a revered elder statesman of the movement.

As an esteemed U.S. Congressman from Georgia, he championed contemporary justice issues like immigration, gun reform, and marriage equality and, in 2016, called for the passage of the Equality Act. This act, crucial to the ongoing fight for equality, prohibits discrimination based on sex, sexual orientation, and gender identity in employment, housing, public accommodations, education, federally funded programs, credit, and jury service. Lewis' oft-repeated quote reminds us that to engage in nonviolent resistance is to "get into good trouble, necessary trouble."

From the 1848 Seneca Falls Convention to the Women's Liberation movement of the 1960s and '70s to the twenty-first-century #MeToo movement, women have fought for freedom—over their votes, bodies, work, and lives. But early on, women of color were excluded, revealing the need for inclusive activism.

STRATEGIES FOR COPING WITH THE IMPACT OF WHAT IS HAPPENING IN OUR WORLD

WOMEN'S SUFFRAGE. Alice Paul and Lucy Burns, among others, vociferously championed women's right to vote and organized the Woman Suffrage Procession, the pièce de résistance of the campaign. The landmark parade of more than 5,000 women marched peacefully from the U.S. Capitol down Pennsylvania Avenue and past the White House on March 3, 1913—the day before Woodrow Wilson's presidential inauguration. The conspicuous endeavor drew extensive publicity and helped garner support for the suffrage movement.

However, there were detractors in vitriolic opposition, inflicting violence upon some one hundred participants, with no police intervention. The police did, however, make arrests of "The Silent Sentinels" who, over a month-long campaign, picketed the White House, holding banners and silently imploring voting rights for women. The arrested suffragists were jailed under brutal treatment at the notorious Occoquan Workhouse in Northern Virginia, where some continued resistance efforts with a hunger strike, subjecting them to violent force-feedings. The publicity surrounding their plight garnered more suffrage support. The President finally relented, but the Nineteenth Amendment wouldn't be ratified until August 18, 1920, its passage the culmination of an arduous journey to voting rights for women.

WOMEN'S LIB. By 1960, women had, in theory, held the right to vote for over four decades. Yet in practice, many were excluded—particularly women of color, who were effectively shut out until the Voting Rights Act of 1965. That same year, Patsy Mink became the first Asian American woman in the U.S. Congress. Still, for many in the Asian American and Pacific Islander community, full enfranchisement didn't arrive until the minority language amendments to the Voting Rights Act were added a decade later, in 1975. Meanwhile, systemic inequality remained deeply entrenched. By 1973, ninety-three women had served in Congress, yet women still couldn't open a bank account or obtain a credit card without a male co-signer—a legal restriction not lifted until 1974.

The Women's Liberation Movement emerged from the second wave of feminism to dismantle patriarchy and secure equality in every aspect of women's lives—from pay equity and educational opportunities to full autonomy and agency.

Through political engagement, policy reform, grassroots activism, anti-discrimination efforts, and advocacy for labor protections, reproductive freedom, women-centered healthcare, and LGBTQIA+ inclusion, the movement

SHARON
PENDANA

pursued women's actualization with peaceful fervor. Its impacts are still felt today in landmark laws, including the Equal Pay Act (1963), Title IX (1972), and the Pregnancy Discrimination Act (1978).

Yet the Equal Rights Amendment (1923) remains unratified after a century, and the repeal of abortion rights once protected by *Roe v. Wade* (1973) marks a troubling authoritarian regression. The fight for gender parity— across race, class, and identity—is far from over. But history shows that legislative victories and social progress are possible when we come together.

THERE IS NO PLANET B.

While industrialization brought modern conveniences, it also unleashed extractive abuses that threaten human health and planetary survival. In response, groups like the Sierra Club emerged, advancing conservation efforts and helping to establish the National Park Service. Its sister agency, the U.S. Forest Service, harnessed the power of messaging with mascots like Smokey Bear ("Only you can prevent forest fires") in the 1940s and Woodsy Owl ("Give a hoot, don't pollute!") during the 1970s anti-pollution wave.

Earth Day began as a 1970 college teach-in. By year's end, President Nixon had signed the Clean Air Act and created the Environmental Protection Agency—measures that improved air quality and added 1.4 years to the average American lifespan within a decade.

Today's environmental justice movements demand

urgent action. Hashtags like #NoDAPL amplify resistance. We must not scroll past destruction—we must act. There is no Planet B.

"MNÍ WIČÓNI" WATER IS LIFE. In 2016, a proposed 1,172-mile pipeline to transport crude oil from North Dakota to Illinois provoked opposition among Indigenous Americans. The pipeline would run beneath the sacred lands of the Standing Rock Sioux and Lake Oahe, their primary water source, violating treaty rights. The youth-led campaign "ReZpect Our Water" popularized the slogan, "Mní Wičóni, Water is Life," on social media.

SHARON
PENDANA

On April 1, Lakota historian LaDonna Brave Bull Allard and fellow water protectors established the Sacred Stone Camp near the pipeline construction site. The encampment, rooted in Indigenous spirituality, became a hub for peaceful protest and prayer space to safeguard the land and water, contributing to the broader No Dakota Access Pipeline (#NoDAPL) movement.

In July, thirty to forty youth from the Standing Rock and Cheyenne River Sioux tribes ran a 2,000-mile relay to Washington, D.C., joined by hundreds along the way, to deliver a petition opposing the pipeline. Their efforts, amplified by the #NoDAPL campaign, brought to light the fight for Indigenous sovereignty, environmental justice, and climate action.

Protestors engaged in civil disobedience, including horseback blockades and chaining themselves to machinery to halt construction and assert their rights. Despite violent responses, they upheld peaceful resistance. In December, the Army Corps of Engineers denied the pipeline's easement at Lake Oahe—a significant win.

In early 2017, the new administration reversed the decision, and by June, oil flowed beneath Lake Oahe. The pipeline completion sparked a national dialogue, calling for accountability and underscoring the need for civic vigilance.

RIGHT OVER MIGHT

Erica Chenoweth, PhD, a Harvard research fellow and now an endowed professor, initially believed revolutionary change required the use of force. After all, the Russian, French, and Algerian revolutions dealt lethal blows to autocratic regimes.

However, her 2006 study, conducted with political scientist Maria J. Stephan, analyzed global resistance campaigns from 1900 to 2006 that involved at least 1,000 participants—and revealed that a bloodless coup is not only possible but also more effective than violent insurgency: twice as likely to succeed and typically four times larger in scope.

Why? Nonviolent resistance has fewer barriers to participation. Violent rebellion often requires physical engagement that deters specific demographics—elderly and disabled individuals, even children.

Though peaceful protests may face violent backlash, their relative safety encourages broader participation. The study found that just 3.5% of a population engaging in sustained unarmed resistance—about eleven million people in the U.S.—can achieve movement goals.

Notably, every campaign that reached this percentage was nonviolent, including Poland's Solidarność and Czechoslovakia's Velvet Revolution. The peaceful oustings of Ferdinand Marcos in the Philippines in 1986 and Slobodan Milošević in Serbia in 2000 prove disruption doesn't have to be deadly.

In the years following the study (2010-2011), frustrated citizens in Tunisia and Egypt used mass occupations, protests, civil disobedience, strikes, digital activism, and street art to disrupt the status quo and overthrow long-standing dictatorial presidencies.

Despite a commitment to peaceful methods, both campaigns faced violent government retaliation, provoking some in the anti-autocracy camp to respond in kind. Still, nonviolent strategies ultimately empowered the people and undermined tyranny. Sustained unrest led to the January 14, 2011, exile of Tunisian President Zine El Abidine Ben Ali and the February 11 ouster of Egyptian President Hosni Mubarak.

And in the U.S., inspired by the 3.5% rule for successful resistance, No Kings emerged as a national day of mass mobilization and anti-authoritarian defiance on June 14, 2025. The date held layered symbolism: Flag Day, the 250th anniversary of the U.S. Army, and the birthday of the sitting President—marked by a planned show of might in the Nation's Capital with a military parade of troops, tanks, and aircraft down Constitution Avenue.

Protesters nationwide saw deep irony in this spectacle, given the administration's increasingly fraught relationship with the Constitution. While armored vehicles rumbled through D.C., Americans gathered in peaceful defiance under a shared tenet: In America, we don't do kings. No thrones. No crowns. No kings.

The dueling optics of power and protest sent a clear message: the people had had enough. What began as a day of action has evolved into a national movement—a coalition of over 200 organizations, including Indivisible, Greenpeace, Planned Parenthood, the ACLU, Color of Change, and everyday Americans, all united to reclaim democracy.

Humans are primed to seek justice, fairness, and equity. When something is amiss, we course correct—or at least try our damnedest to. History abounds with courageous acts of resistance against overwhelming odds: fighting injustice without force. From Gandhi's Satyagraha against colonial rule to the global reckoning of the MeToo movement, we've witnessed how collective mobilization—across lines of race, class, gender, and more—can drive profound change. Let us embrace that intersectionality. The future is ours to shape.

Resistance arises in response to tyranny, colonization, oppression, discrimination, exploitation, and all the -isms. Nonviolent resistance begins with courage, conviction, and the commitment to confront Goliath—without the slingshot.

Sharon Pendana is the author of *Secret Washington, D.C.:*
An Unusual Guide (Jonglez Publishing, 2025). As the
founder of *The Trove*, she writes about the fascinating
journeys of remarkable creatives, highlighting the things
they treasure. Among the treasures Sharon holds dear
are her freedoms and the right to advocate for positive
change. You might find her at a protest near you.

Chapter 15

What to Do When the World Goes Crazy

By SHERRY KAPPEL

"Not everything that is faced can be changed;
but nothing can be changed until it is faced."

—JAMES BALDWIN

THIS BOOK HAS covered centuries of history, in America and across the globe; now it's your turn to make some!

At times it can seem like the world is spiraling out of control, everyone is filled with hate and vitriol, people are being unfairly hurt or even killed, and nobody seems to be doing much about it.

Maybe you're in a demographic that doesn't typically get targeted (at least, yet), but you see others who are. Maybe people around you can't afford food or healthcare, or they're struggling in the aftermath of a natural disaster and no one is supporting them. And you may want to help but you're not sure how and you're stressed and running scared. Do you fight for them? Do you kneel and pray? Or do you shut your eyes, hunker down, and wait for the smoke to clear like the hazy tendrils of a very bad dream?

We all know the World War II poem by Pastor Martin Niemöller, but read it again—as if new:

> *First they came for the Communists*
> *And I did not speak out*
> *Because I was not a Communist*
> *Then they came for the Socialists*
> *And I did not speak out*
> *Because I was not a Socialist*
> *Then they came for the trade unionists*
> *And I did not speak out*
> *Because I was not a trade unionist*
> *Then they came for the Jews*
> *And I did not speak out*
> *Because I was not a Jew*
> *Then they came for me*
> *And there was no one left*
> *To speak out for me*

Each demographic being demonized is a stepping-stone to the next one. *None of us* can afford to think we're safe in a fascist regime—and our humanity also requires us to support other people in need. But what does it mean to provide support or speak out? If rich, powerful, famous people are shouting from the rooftops about current events and *they* aren't making much difference, how can *you*?

That's exactly what those who would silence you want you to think. That's why they're constantly trying to overwhelm you and limit free speech, the right to protest, and who can vote. Fascists know their limitations, and they know they can't win against a loud majority. Because each of us may be only one tiny individual amongst 340 million Americans, but collectively we are huge, loud, and strong. Grave injustices never last forever, but the more people know and the more they protest, the sooner these injustices end. So let's get started!

SHERRY
KAPPEL

POLITICS ARE PERSONAL

Remember "the good old days" when everyone said, "It's just politics," as if most of what was said or done in D.C. made very little difference in our everyday lives, and people could disagree but still be friends? Perhaps a bit belatedly, we've come to realize just how much power legislators have over the freedoms we've histori-cally taken for granted and the direct impact that power has on the quality of our lives, as well as the underlying moral differences that can lead a person to support one candidate over another.

While elected officials might not always feel the need to keep their campaign promises or support the constituents who elected them, they do typically want to stay in office or even continue to climb the political ladder; some even worry about their legacy. Never discount the power we have over them! When we're quiet, they're happy to focus on the wishes of their party and the lobbyists who drop money in their laps. When we become the proverbial squeaky wheel, however, they sit up and start to listen. There are numerous ways to get their attention.

CALL, WRITE, EMAIL, TEXT, VISIT. REPEAT. Contact your representatives to let them know how you feel about the issues—and not just the reps and the issues in the national news, but your local reps, as well. (Too many people ignore their local politicians, but this is where things start!) Be polite, but firm and precise. Cite as many facts and details as possible. Let them know you're monitoring how they vote, you know when they lie, and you're holding them accountable. Not feeling eloquent? Use automated systems such as Resistbot that will contact them for you.

SHOW UP IN EVERY POSSIBLE FORUM. Attend townhalls, as well as school board meetings, rallies, fundraisers, and anything else your representatives might be at; even if they're not always going to show, they *will* hear all about it and the news will almost certainly talk about it. Plan what you're going to say, as speaking time is limited and every word counts.

STILL UNHAPPY? KICK THEM OUT! Campaign for opposition candidates. Or campaign for same-party candidates who are more forceful and willing to fight for what's right. Get on the phone to other voters, go door to door, put up signs, or whatever else a candidate might need. Rest assured their office will have ideas. Or even run for office yourself! Everybody must start somewhere, and if you're motivated by doing what's right for everyone, people will see it and respond.

VOTE, VOTE, VOTE. Americans have had it so good the past few decades compared to many countries, that we've become very complacent about the privilege of voting. The Pew Research Center says that although voter turnout in the U.S. has soared in the past several elections, America still ranks only thirty-first among the fifty countries they studied. We cannot afford to sit back any longer and let others decide who will lead us—far too much is at stake. And don't let your friends and family be complacent, either; it's simply not acceptable (and really never was).

Consider, too, how groups dealing with bigotry are being victimized by gerrymandering and other methodologies to keep their votes from counting. Think about how they're being affected, listen to their concerns, and recognize that even if you don't like the price of gas,

SHERRY
KAPPEL

for example, far more basic American rights are being threatened and need your protection. And even if you don't understand or share a group's concerns, as Pastor Niemöller pointed out, those who would take away the rights of one group would just as easily take away the rights of another. A fascist doesn't really care about any of us; separating us into groups is simply a method for sparking division and dissent—divide and conquer. Vote for the rights and freedoms of *all* Americans!

SPEAK UP & SHARE THE TRUTH

There is literally nothing more powerful than your voice, especially when armed with the truth. Philosophers have long espoused that in the marketplace of ideas, the truth is superior and will rise to the top when freedom of speech is protected. This is why authoritarians and other politicians with questionable motives lie so loudly and continuously, denigrate public education and the teaching of history, ban books they disagree with, and even discourage public gatherings: *keep the masses ignorant*, lest the truth shall set them free.

SUPPORT YOUR ARGUMENTS WITH FACTS. Educate yourself as much as possible. If one is to call out another for spreading falsehoods, one needs to make every effort to be accurate. While people tend to think of those who disagree as stupid or clueless, some are very good at gaslighting; and twisting your words limit their opportunities.

224

Follow fair-minded journalists and other experts online like Joy Reid, Heather Cox Richardson, Robert Reich, Dan Rather, and more to refine your views and see which arguments and verbiage resonate most.

Now you're armed and ready to push back when other people state falsehoods. However, don't lose your cool—don't be petty or let your emotions get the best of you. This doesn't mean you can't be passionate, just let the facts speak more loudly than, say, name calling. It can be hard to do when the other person is being loud or hateful but know that you'll be even more impressive if you maintain your dignity. (And remember, it's not always about changing the other person's mind, but rather influencing others who are listening in.)

Beyond the issues at hand, call out situations where people normalize unacceptable behavior. If, for example, a president skips over congressional approvals or an official defies a court order, it isn't just about that specific issue; it's breaking down the rule of law Americans agreed upon in a better time, and more generally the checks and balances our country runs on. So even if someone might agree with the particular view sparking the defiance, you need to point out that there's much more at stake. While many people have concerns about immigration rates, for instance, this shouldn't make it acceptable to treat immigrants inhumanely.

PUT IT ALL IN WRITING. Putting your thoughts in writing is a special activity that allows you to clarify your positioning, add and refine your reasoning, then share it far and wide—perhaps even building a following that further shares and expands on your verbiage.

If you're not practiced or comfortable putting your thoughts on paper, you can start by signing petitions. There are dozens of petition aggregators, and some of them allow you to add a comment. Feeling brave? Contribute your own petition on a subject you're passionate about! Similarly, respond to articles and editorials. Join online groups like "Suburban Women and Beyond for a Better America" on Facebook and build a social following. As you get more comfortable, write your own articles and letters to the editor.

VOTE WITH YOUR WALLET / SPEAK WITH YOUR MONEY. Money talks, particularly to those at the top of the food chain; many corporate heads have donated a fair sum of money to one candidate or another and their donations are typically part of the public record. You can find all sorts of information online about who does or does not support DEI, for example, or whether their management team agrees with you politically. For a quick summary of political spending, download the free Goods United Us / "GUU" app. Check out the businesses you frequent, then tell a good—or bad—company why you're now spending more with them or less than you have in the past.

YOU ARE NOT ALONE: PARTNER WITH OTHERS

As traumatic as political and cultural turmoil can feel, getting to know others who share your feelings can alleviate some of the stress and help you retain your faith in humanity. *You are not alone!* Meeting like-minded people online is great; in person is even better. There are dozens, if not hundreds, of very active national and local groups. Just a couple that come to mind are Indivisible, and Red, Wine & Blue. Each group is slightly different, with a somewhat different focus, range of activities, and level of involvement. Find your people and your niche and get involved.

AND YES, PROTEST. The majority of Americans have had the luxury of little real experience with protesting. At most they've marched in convivial rallies with like-minded people while the local police looked tolerantly on. And while most group events continue to be peaceful, the ones that make the news can be scary. Protests are, however, a very powerful tool that impress with their solidarity and the sheer numbers.

Author and Zen teacher Peter Coyote taught a class at Harvard on protesting. He describes the event as an invitation to a better world for those observing, and a ceremony—and no one accepts a ceremonial invitation when you're being screamed at. He states that, "You have to know who the real audience of the protest is. The audience is NEVER the police, the politicians, the Board of supervisors, Congress, etc. The audience is always the American people, who are trying to decide who they can trust; who will not embarrass them. If you win them, you win power at the box office and power to make positive change."

227

He goes on to outline strategies for ensuring a positive outcome, particularly around the advantages of appearing as neat, clean, patriotic, and non-violent as possible. His suggestions include dressing with respect for the occasion, letting your signs do all the talking, limiting your protests to the daylight, and carrying an American flag—it's all about the optics.

Most critically, *be peaceful*. "True pacifism," or "non-violent resistance," the Rev. Dr. Martin Luther King Jr. wrote in *Stride Toward Freedom*, is "a courageous confrontation of evil by the power of love." More specifically, do not engage with anyone who gets violent, especially as they are quite possibly provocateurs who don't even believe in your cause and want to make you look bad. Coyote notes: "The American people are watching and once again if we behave in ways that can be misinterpreted, we'll watch this explained to the public in [opposition] videos benefiting [the very people] who started the turmoil. So wake up. Vent at home. In public practice discipline and self-control."

Despite the concerns, remember that most protests are a joyful sharing of empathy and humanity with good people. I've attended many, a lot of them with my daughters and friends, and we all found them all very uplifting.

PRIORITIZE PEOPLE OF COLOR. One final note on group activities, particularly rallies and protests: if you're a white person, bear in mind that there are other demographics with a lot more on the line—and, therefore, a lot more experience protesting. Take advantage of opportunities to better understand your Black and Brown brothers and sisters, the struggles they've faced in our culture, and to learn the most effective methods of resistance. Also, be aware that the police are much more likely to use weapons and even lethal force against Black protesters. Keep an eye out and help protect them! Some other important notes:

1. Do your research on racism, *before* you engage. There are scores of excellent books and movies on the subject; you don't need to absorb them all before getting to work but having a solid foundation demonstrates respect. And while some Black people are happy to answer your questions, it's not their responsibility to educate white folks, and they do it far too often.

2. Listen to Black voices without interrupting—respect their lived experiences even if you don't fully understand them. There have been several moments in my journey where I questioned their perspective, but ultimately, I grasped where they were coming from because I set aside my biases and really listened.

3. Use your learnings for self-reflection! Even if you've been involved in efforts around supporting People of Color, the simple fact is that racism is hard coded into everything in our culture—so accept that at some point you'll be called out for doing or saying something racist. As author and educator bell hooks states, "When liberal white

folks fail to understand how they can and/or do embody white supremacist values and beliefs even though they may not embrace racism . . . they cannot recognize the ways their actions support and affirm the very structure of racist domination and oppression that they wish to see eradicated." So listen, learn, and emerge a better person.

Peter Coyote comments that he learned what he knows about protesting by watching Dr. King and the civil rights protests of the 1950s and '60s. "It was the discipline and courage of African-Americans that drew such a clear line in the American sand that people were forced to take sides and that produced the Civil Rights Act."

BE CREATIVE

While putting yourself out there, either physically or verbally, is one of the most effective ways to resist authoritarianism and influence others, it's not for everyone. If arguing with strangers makes you physically ill, other alternatives exist. There are many, many stories from the past on how people quietly supported others and fought against unjust systems, some of which have already been mentioned earlier in this book.

World War II alone is rife with such stories. People found ways to hide their Jewish neighbors or even support their escape to safer places. When commanded to make bombs for the Nazis, Czech workers produced duds. And when assembly line workers at French auto-maker Renault were forced to make equipment for the Nazis, they quietly slowed down production, introduced faulty parts, and started sabotaging oil gages so that German vehicles had engine issues.

In other words: be creative! What do you do for a living? Do you have an exceptional skill, or work someplace like Renault? While hopefully you're not manufacturing bombs, think of ways to put your talents to use in support of others' rights and freedoms.

DRAW ON YOUR HUMANITY

It's a scary world we're living in right now and you may find acts of resistance scary as well, but at the end of the day, the goal is a kinder, more loving society; never lose sight of that. Make sure you take care of others along the way, especially those in targeted demographics, for example People of Color, immigrants, LGBTQIA+, the elderly, and people living with disabilities.

A harder task is resisting the urge to be like "them"—those who are willfully ignorant and motivated by hate. Do not become what you're fighting against! Focus on the message versus the messenger. It might help to understand that their negativity inhibits their life experiences and the full scope of what it means to be human (not to mention how their choice of politicians most likely limits their own rights, their healthcare, and much more). It's easy to say "they deserve what they get," but regardless of whatever else might occur, your empathy, dignity, and love for others will allow you to get more from this life than they ever will, unless or until they choose to change. And people *do* change, especially if you demonstrate a better way of being.

Also recognize that you need to practice self-care *and* pushing yourself further than perhaps you've ever gone—and it's a difficult balance. These times call for everyone concerned about the future of humanity to step outside their comfort zone and do more than they'd once imagined doing not so long ago. Only you can determine your limits, but you might find that you have more grit than you knew. As James Baldwin observed, "Once you realize that you can do something, it would be difficult to live with yourself if you didn't do it."

Bottom line: *Love yourself, and love one another.*

Sherry Kappel is a poet, essayist, and fiction writer with an MFA from the University of Pittsburgh. She looks for the best in humanity and is driven by empathy in her writing and in life. Her work is on Medium, where she also edits Snapshots, the Haiku Hub, and special projects for Our Human Family. Sherry lives in North Carolina with her husband, daughters, and critters.

AFTERWORD

By Stephen Matlock

WELL ... THAT WAS quite a ride, wasn't it? These essays come from a variety of people with different viewpoints, life experiences, and passions, yet they all seem to convey the same message: something is very, very wrong with this world, and it needs to be set right, right away!

You might feel overwhelmed right now because you feel—like many people of good heart—that it is all too much, that everything demands action right away, that every warning light is flashing red, that every voice is raised in the cacophony of terror and anger and fear, drowning out the sense of your own self to see what's happening and step back for a moment to just . . . breathe. To appreciate that you are alive.

Yes, it is a battle just to stay alive. Jobs are vanishing. Prices are skyrocketing. Adults and children are being kidnapped and taken to torture camps. Black women are being terminated from their government jobs at much higher rates than other groups. Black voices are being silenced in the media, in education, in science. Universities are under tremendous pressure to end any semblance of fairness and equity for Black, Indigenous, and People of Color. And the public is under great pressure to deny science.

We're all just trying to hang on, you know . . .

But that feeling of "it is all too much!" is an entirely natural reaction to a world with more than eight billion people trying, like you and me, to find their way to better their lives and their children's lives.

So what is needed, right now, is for you to find your center. What are your ways of finding peace? Of knowing who you are and what you can do?

What's needed is not reacting but first contemplating your values: What are you here for, and what do you want to see become better in your world?

Is it your own peace? Is it prosperity for your community? Is it safety for your family? Hope for a change in our current crises that could be solved if people just acted decently? A few people to be the adults in the room to address social, economic, and environmental disasters that threaten to end this thing we call "our world"?

The call that "we must make this better" comes from our human identity. From us.

And we are all tasked with the care of our shared siblings—our human family, as it were. And in doing that care, not everyone does everything, and not everything that is done is done exactly the same way every time.

Because you are here to be you. Whatever your passions are. Whatever your hopes are. Whatever it is that is in you that cries out, "I am here!"

It is enough that you are moved to consider what to do next. It is enough that you are motivated to reach out to like-minded people to strategize about an act of courage or rebellion. It is enough that you show up for a protest, that you show up at an ICE raid, that you show up in a court, that you show up to protect your neighbor. Every action you take, big or small, adds to the giant movement of people who want a better world.

STEPHEN MATLOCK

Trust me on this: No action is too small to matter.

I know of people who, in their six or seven decades of existence, have never participated in so much as writing a letter to the editor but who now have gone to their first public protest. Some are moved to join a service club to help people struggling with food security. Some provide water and sandwiches for protestors. Some form circles of community engaged in a common activity together, where they also talk about issues and strategize how to use their privileges and freedom to agitate for change in public forums. Change comes from people becoming engaged in their passions to heal the wounds of this world.

Perhaps those who are identified as "We the People" have not yet fully roused themselves from slumber, but the people are waking up, taking a good look at our situation, and they are getting mad and getting ready to do something.

Your heart will guide you. Your connections will form. Your path will become clear.

All it takes is that step. Who knows where the journey will take you?

And when you do take a step, please let us know what you're doing. It's great to find out what everyone is doing to make this world a place for everyone in our human family.

Stephen Matlock (retired) is a part-time author and gardener in the Pacific Northwest, often overwhelmed by both words and weeds. He has been writing about his journey into inclusion and diversity for close to twenty years. In his extra time, he volunteers at the local food bank, has lively conversations in Haitian Creole with his friends on the island, and works in his town to build a liveable community for all.

ABOUT STEPHEN MATLOCK

ACKNOWLEDGMENTS

THIS ANTHOLOGY, REPRESENTING innumerable hours of dedication and insight, would not have been possible without the invaluable contributions of many individuals. Heartfelt gratitude is extended to each person who offered their expertise, time, and support to bring these diverse voices together within these pages.

First, appreciation is extended to the talented authors whose chapters are the beating heart and soul of this collection. Their dedication to their craft and willingness to share their personal narratives, despite potention personal and professional risk for some, speaks volumes of their courage and love for humanity.

Sincere thanks go to the Our Human Family editorial team:

- Sherry Kappel, for her insightful guidance during the editing process
- Stephen Matlock, for his unwavering commitment to accuracy, detail, and clarity
- Todd Wilson, whose design aesthetic always challenges me to push the design
- Joe Petrovich, for believing

Acknowledgment is also given to the Our Human Family Board of Directors who provided crucial support at different stages throughout this project.

Finally, thanks to family and friends for the time, space, and nurturance to create throughout this demanding but rewarding journey. Their belief in this project and their unwavering support have been a constant source of motivation.

It is hoped that this anthology will spark dialogue, inspire reflection, and move readers to strengthen their resilience through their unique expression of resistance. Thank you for joining in this intellectual adventure.

NOTES

For CHAPTER 1

1. Robert J. Pushaw Jr. "Ulysses S. Grant and the Lost Opportunity for Racial Justice." (2018). Accessed 5/5/2025. https://constitutionalcommentary.lib.umn.edu/article/ulysses-s-grant-and-the-lost-opportunity-for-racial-justice/#:~:text=Perhaps%2520most%2520significantly%252C%2520Grant%2520ardently,685%252C%2520744%252C%2520856).

2. Ron Elving. "Dixie's Long Journey From Democratic Stronghold To Republican Redoubt." It's All Politics. (6/25/2015). Accessed 5/5/2025. https://www.npr.org/sections/itsallpolitics/2015/06/25/417154906/dixies-long-journey-from-democratic-stronghold-to-republican-redoubt.

3. "How Groups Voted in 1976." Roper Center for Public Opinion Research. Accessed 5/5/2025. https://ropercenter.cornell.edu/how-groups-voted-1976.

4. Saladin Ambar. "Woodrow Wilson: Life Before the Presidency." Accessed 5/5/2025. https://millercenter.org/president/wilson/life-before-the-presidency.

5. President Wilson House. Accessed 5/5/2025. https://woodrowwilsonhouse.org/wilson-topics/wilson-and-race/.

6. Ibid.

7. "Lesson 5: Eleanor Roosevelt and the Rise of Social Reform in the 1930s." Accessed 5/5/2025. https://edsitement.neh.gov/lesson-plans/lesson-5-eleanor-roosevelt-and-rise-social-reform-1930s.

8. "Africal American Railroad Workers." Golden Spike National Historical Park. (2024). Accessed 5/5/2025. https://www.nps.gov/gosp/learn/historyculture/african-american-railroad-workers.htm.

9. Larry DeWitt. "The Decision to Exclude Agricultural and Domestic Workers from the 1935 Social Security Act." (2010). Accessed 5/5/2025. https://www.ssa.gov/policy/docs/ssb/v70n4/v70n4p49.html.

10. Mark Engler and Paul Engler. "The 'Make Me Do It' Myth." (2021). Accessed 5/5/2025. https://www.dissentmagazine.org/online_articles/the-make-me-do-it-myth/.

11. A. J. Baime, The Accidental President: Harry S. Truman and the Four Months That Changed the World (Boston: Mariner Books, 2018).

12. "The Truman Doctrine and the Marshall Plan." Accessed 5/5/2025. https://history.state.gov/departmenthistory/short-history/truman.

13. "Executive Order 9981: Desegregation of the Armed Forces (1948)." Milestone Documents. Accessed 5/5/2025. https://www.archives.gov/milestone-documents/executive-order-9981.

14. "John F. Kennedy's Legacy Resides in African-American History." Harvard Political Review. (2013). Accessed 5/5/2025. https://theharvardpoliticalreview.com/john-f-kennedys-legacy-resides-african-american-history/.

15. Ibid.

16. Rita Braver. "LBJ and his monumental presidency." CBS News. (2023). Accessed 5/5/2025. https://www.cbsnews.com/news/lbj-lyndon-johnson-and-his-monumental-presidency/.

17. Ibid.

18. "Biography: Lyndon B. Johnson." LBJ Presidential Library. Accessed 5/5/2025. https://www.lbjlibrary.org/life-and-legacy/the-man-himself/biography.

19. Ibid.

20. "Lyndon B. Johnson." Wikipedia. Accessed 5/5/2025. https://en.wikipedia.org/wiki/Lyndon_B._Johnson.

21. Ibid.

22. "89th United States Congress." Wikipedia. Accessed 5/5/2025. https://en.wikipedia.org/wiki/89th_United_States_Congress.

23. Charles Kaiser. "'We may have lost the south': what LBJ really said about Democrats in 1964." The Guardian (2023). Accessed 5/5/2025. https://www.theguardian.com/books/2023/jan/22/we-may-have-lost-the-south-lbj-democrats-civil-rights-act-1964-bill-moyers.

24. Gene Demby. "Who is the White Vote?" All Things Considered. (2020). Accessed 5/5/2025. https://www.npr.org/2020/11/05/931836604/who-is-the-white-vote.

25. "Southern strategy." Wikipedia. Accessed 5/5/2025. https://en.wikipedia.org/wiki/Southern_strategy.

26. Mark Engler. "Dog-Whistle Politics: Talking About Race Without Talking About Race." Morningside Center for Teaching Social Responsibility. (2016). Accessed 5/5/2025. https://www.morningsidecenter.org/teachable-moment/lessons/dog-whistle-politics-talking-about-race-without-talking-about-race.

27. Ibid.

28. Robert Brent Toplin. "Dog-Whistle Politics: It's a Tradition with the GOP." History News Network. (2015). Accessed 5/5/2025. https://www.historynewsnetwork.org/article/dog-whistle-politics-its-a-tradition-with-the-gop.

29. Earl Black, The Vital South: How Presidents Are Elected (Cambridge, MA: Harvard University Press, 1992).

30. Alabama, Arkansas, Georgia, Louisiana, Mississippi

31. "George Wallace's 1963 Inaugural Address." Wikipedia. Accessed 5/5/2025. https://en.wikipedia.org/wiki/George_Wallace's_1963_Inaugural_Address.

32. Dan T. Carter, From George Wallace to Newt Gingrich: Race in the Conservative Counterrevolution, 1963–1994 (Baton Rouge: Louisiana State University Press, 1996).

33. Tom van der Voort. "Watergate: The Break-in." UVA Miller Center. Accessed 5/5/2025. https://millercenter.org/the-presidency/educational-resources/watergate/watergate-break.

34. Jordan Moran. "Nixon and the Pentagon Papers." UVA Miller Center. Accessed 5/5/2025. https://millercenter.org/the-presidency/educational-resources/first-domino-nixon-and-the-pentagon-papers.

35. "The Campaign Ad that Reshaped Criminal Justice." The Takeaway. (2015). Accessed 5/5/2025. https://www.wnycstudios.org/podcasts/takeaway/segments/crime-reshaped-criminal-justice.

36. Ibid.

37. Ibid.

38. "Gravely Ill, Atwater Offers Apology." New York Times. (1991). Accessed 5/5/2025. https://www.nytimes.com/1991/01/13/us/gravely-ill-atwater-offers-apology.html.

39. Anthony Zurcher. "The birth of the Obama 'birther' conspiracy." BBC News. (2016). Accessed 5/5/2025. https://www.bbc.com/news/election-us-2016-37391652.

40. Amber Phillips. "'They're rapists.' President Trump's campaign launch speech two years later, annotated." The Washington Post. (2017). Accessed 5/5/2025. https://www.washingtonpost.com/news/the-fix/wp/2017/06/16/theyre-rapists-presidents-trump-campaign-launch-speech-two-years-later-annotated/.

41. The White House. "President Trump is Removing Killers, Rapists and Drug Dealers from Our Streets." (2025). Accessed 5/5/2025. https://www.whitehouse.gov/articles/2025/03/president-trump-is-removing-killers-rapists-and-drug-dealers-from-our-streets/

42. "Robert Bork's America." Wikisource. Accessed 5/5/2025. https://en.wikisource.org/wiki/Robert_Bork%27s_America.

42. Charlton D. McIlwain and Stephen M. Caliendo, "Mitt Romney's Racist Appeals: How Race Was Played in the 2012 Presidential Election," American Behavioral Scientist 58, no. 9 (2014), https://doi.org/10.1177/0002764213506212.

Brainy Quote. Accessed 5/5/2025. https://www.brainyquote.com/quotes/will_rogers_122697.

Mike Allen. "RNC Chief to Say It Was 'Wrong' to Exploit Racial Conflict for Votes." The Washington Post. (2005). Accessed 5/5/2025. https://www.washingtonpost.com/wp-dyn/content/article/2005/07/13/AR2005071302342.html.

NOTES

ABOUT

Our Human Family

OUR HUMAN FAMILY has been fostering conversations about achieving racial equity since April 2019. Our goal is to unite the world—our world, our sphere of influence—by dispelling the lie of race and the practice of bigotry and replacing them with the truth of love.

If you have been enlightened or inspired by our writers' works, intended to broaden perspectives and foster empathy and compassion, then your membership to the digital publication *OHF Weekly* (ohfweekly.com) will provide unlimited access to the narratives we publish.

The advocacy of Our Human Family, Inc., a 501(c)(3) charitable organization, manifests in creating and offering workshops, panel discussion groups, hosting guest speaker events, and much more.

We understand that there is no one-size-fits-all approach to people. The same applies to providing the various segments of our customer base with the knowledge and skills necessary to eradicate racism. We make this possible by creating informative and transformative materials that will evolve with the times and meet the specific needs of various segments of our audience.

The subject of racism is broad and complicated. Its components required close examination and nuanced explanation. While our message is singular, we must tailor our conversations and presentations to bring awareness to these aspects. These items must also be updated to reflect current challenges.

We cannot do the work of racial equity, allyship, and inclusion without the support of people like you. In the same way that it takes a village to raise a child, it will take all of us to end racism and create a more equitable world. Our Human Family, Inc. is working to bring an end to racism and establish a society rooted in equitable outcomes for all.

You can help us continue our anti-racism work. Please support the critical work and word of Our Human Family at the forefront of the national conversation by making a tax-deductible donation at *ourhumanfamily. org/contribute.*

Love one another.

LOVE ONE ANOTHER.

www.ingramcontent.com/pod-product-compliance
Lightning Source LLC
Chambersburg PA
CBHW021713120626
46545CB00004B/1543